CREATING CLOTHES FOR DOLLS

How to achieve that
perfect fit and authentic look

Joan Nerini

TAFFETA PUBLICATIONS

CONTENTS

NICOLA

Joan Nerini © 1982

DOLLS PAPER PATTERNS

For illustrated catalogue of current range, please send stamped addressed envelope to:

JOAN NERINI
c/o TAFFETA PUBLICATIONS
PO BOX 1307
LONDON W5 1DN

These patterns are based on styles from the Victorian and Edwardian era. There are designs for girl, boy and baby dolls as well as fashion outfits for lady dolls, and include underwear and hats. They fit dolls from 8"-30" (20cm-76cm) with more than one size included in many of the patterns together with alternative suggestions for flexibility of use to achieve that perfect fit.

Text: Joan Nerini © Copyright 1987
Illustrations: Frances Nerini © Copyright 1987
Design and Layout: Ferini Designs, Lowestoft, Suffolk
Typeset by: Kos Associates, London

First edition printed in Great Britain 1987
by Anglia Design & Print Services Ltd for Taffeta Publications
PO Box 1307, London W5 1DN

ISBN 0 9512835 0 2

Front Cover: Illustrations extracted from The Queen, The Lady's Newspaper, 1875 and Victorian Fashions & Costumes from Harper's Bazar: 1867-1898. (Dover Publications, Inc. New York)

FOREWORD

Dressing so many various dolls, publishing the NICOLA patterns and now writing and producing this book could not have been achieved without the help and advice of so many doll collectors and enthusiasts, each one allowing me to learn more and more about dolls and every aspect of their clothes.

I am especially grateful to:

David & Jo Barrington of Yesterday Child
Yvonne Bentley
Gillie & John Charlson
Carol Jackman of Recollect
Jackie Jacobs
Pat Lawson
Carole & Bill Parrish of Sheer Elegance
Carol & Debbie Stanton of Living Dolls
Peter Stockham of Images & his wife, Ann
Marlis Tabizel
Countess Maree Tarnowska
and
Babs & Stan Tomlinson

My grateful thanks also go to my daughter Frances for her constant encouragement and artistic help not only with the patterns but also the illustrations and design of this book.

INTRODUCTION

How it all began

I have always lived in a creative and artistic environment, my mother teaching my sister and I to sew, knit and crochet at an early age.

My mother later became a knitwear designer and my father had a lifetime hobby with model railways, exhibiting and winning recognition for the fine detail and workmanship of his trains and the landscapes in which they were displayed. Marrying an artist and having two children whose own artistic talents flourished, I suppose I should not be too surprised that my own hobby of sewing and dressmaking has now developed in such a creative way.

I was first introduced to the wonderful world of dolls and their clothes when I met Yvonne Bentley in the late 70's and through her met Countess Maree Tarnowska whose help and advice in the early days was invaluable. So my dressmaking skills took a change of direction, adapting them to the reduced scale of dolls clothes. I became fascinated by the miniature proportions of the clothes that still needed the correct positioning of pattern pieces on fabric, the cutting out and then making-up so that skirts hung gracefully, the fullness of gathers or pleats were proportioned to the style of dress, and the exact fitting of bodices and sleeves, all to reveal the charm of each individual doll.

As I dressed more and more dolls, using authentic old fabric, trimmings and lace - whether it was my own design or a faithfully reproduced copy of an original, cut to fit the measurements of a particular doll - my expertise grew.

In dressing collector's dolls, I worked only from the measurements of a doll, never wishing to take a doll away from the owner for safety reasons as well as my own peace of mind. From these measurements I would prepare miniature pattern pieces and make up a sample in some less precious material, especially if the antique fabric to be used was only just enough to complete the dress.

All this led me to research the different fabrics which would have been available in the nineteenth century as well as the trimmings, lace and even fastenings. I learnt not only about dolls' fashions, reading books and studying the clothes in museums and private collections, but also researched Victorian and Edwardian children's and adult fashions discovering how their construction and styles differed so much from our present day clothes.

The NICOLA Dolls Paper Patterns

With the growing interest in craftwork and especially dolls and dollmaking, there has developed a great interest in dolls' clothes that reflect that 'old fashioned look'.

While many dollmakers are also experienced dressmakers, it is often very time consuming for them to think out and create period styled clothes for their dolls. Even the individual doll dressmakers or the busy mother wishing to dress her children's dolls in something different, can find the help of a commercial pattern most welcome. While there were some patterns for period styled dolls clothes available in this country a few years back, the majority were being imported from overseas. I therefore decided to make use of all those pattern pieces I had accumulated and prepare commercial patterns for dolls clothes with the 'old fashioned look'. With the help of my daughter, Frances, who provided the artistic layout, illustrations and liaison with the printers, I started to publish the NICOLA Dolls Paper Patterns. By popular demand and by listening to requests such as "Have you a pattern for a dress similar to this?" or "Will you be bringing out a similar pattern in a larger or smaller size?", I have continued to add more and more designs to the range of patterns. In order to give the doll dressmaker more flexibility with these patterns, I included pattern pieces for more than one size of garment as well as alternative suggestions to adapt a pattern to another style, such as using a basic Norfolk jacket pattern for a boy doll, and by recutting the neckline, adding a squared collar and omitting the vertical bands, converting it to become a jacket for a sailor outfit.

Becoming known for the NICOLA patterns, it was not long before I was being asked to talk about doll costuming and - like the seminars that teach the art of dollmaking - I started to give courses and workshop demonstrations to teach the intricacies of sewing for the smaller scale of dolls clothes and the different approach needed in their construction to give that authentic look.

This book has really evolved from the many questions I am constantly being asked about how to achieve that perfect fit and authentic look. Whereas the content of this book can be used to complement the NICOLA Dolls Paper Patterns or any other commercial pattern you may be using, it can also serve as a guide for you to create your own patterns.

Where should I measure my doll and why chose that particular part to measure?

Chapter 1 shows you where to measure your doll, with the guidance of a Measurement and Outline Body chart identifying all the various areas of a doll's body in alphabetical sequence. I then describe the various construction details that are significant for each individual measurement in the same alphabetical sequence for ease of reference.

How can I adapt a pattern if it is too big (or too small)?

INTRODUCTION - continued

How do I alter the pattern in only one or two areas without spoiling the rest of the construction of the garment? You then ask.

As dolls vary so much in shape and size, there is bound to be a time when a commercial pattern, although correct for the height of a doll could be too big or too small in the separate proportions that make up the height or width. There is of course the grid system to enlarge or reduce the outline of the pattern pieces on evenly squared paper. This will be satisfactory providing you know that your doll is an exact size larger or smaller than the pattern. It may be, however, that after measuring your doll and comparing the measurements with the same area on the paper pattern, you find that alteration is only needed in one or two areas.

Chapter 2 'Altering your Pattern' is divided into headings to cover the logical sequence of constructing your doll's garment from the bodice through to the sleeve and neckline to adding the skirt, etc., as it is easier to alter the pattern in sections rather than pin the whole pattern together and try on the complete garment. Also you will be able to find individual problem areas in a particular section more easily. In the form of Questions and Answers following the same sequence of measurements throughout the doll's body, I have listed all the possible problem areas and given a variety of solutions to alter the pattern to fit your doll.

All the solutions are accompanied by diagramatical illustrations to show you exactly where to make the alteration. Because a pattern has to be altered in a different way when it needs to be either enlarged or reduced, I have further divided these possible problem areas into two sections - "If the Pattern is Too Big", followed by "If the Pattern is Too Small".

It may be that you have never attempted to alter a pattern, using it exactly and discovering all too late that the neckline is too large causing the bodice to sag, or that the shoulders are too wide causing the sleeves to appear too long and cover the doll's hands. Or even more disastrously, it is too small and you cannot even get the dress over the doll's head or the sleeves past its hands.

I hope that these two beginning chapters will encourage you to check the pattern pieces and attempt to make the necessary alterations before you start sewing. This is especially important if you are dressing an antique doll with just enough antique fabric to complete the outfit and with nothing in reserve for last minute alterations. Even if you did have extra fabric in reserve, the older the fabric the more likely it is that the stitching will leave a definite imprint and any unpicking of seams and further correction could be very noticeable.

INTRODUCTION - continued

What fabric should I chose? Where can I find antique fabric and how do I make the best use of it? When and where should I use lace, and/or braid and ribbons? What fastening should I use? are all natural follow-on questions.

Choosing your fabric and its colour, the complimentary trimmings and lace are all a matter of very personal taste. I hope that my notes on fabric, lace, trimmings and different fastenings you can use, will help you decide what to look for, where to find them, and how to use them to the best advantage. Whatever you yourself feel is right will, I am sure, give you much pleasure in making up the clothes and seeing your doll wearing your handiwork.

I am often asked for more detailed step-by-step advice on certain aspects of the general construction of dolls' clothes. Whilst it is appreciated that it is the confined space on the pages of a commercial pattern that dictates how condensed the making-up instructions will be and that doll dressmakers experienced with making adult clothes are assumed to be familiar with general sewing techniques and that a novice could find out about such basic techniques from a sewing manual, it is the reduced scale of such clothes that presents a different approach to these skills.

How do you fit a neckband to the abrupt curve of a doll's neckline without puckering the crossway binding right in the front where it would be most noticeable; or set a sleeve into the small circle of a doll's armhole when those with even the slimmest hand and fingers find such a confined space difficult to manipulate? Also many of the more elaborate French style dresses contain constructional detail which reflects the former era they represent and are not necessarily skills used in adult or even dolls clothes of today.

I hope therefore that all the general sewing techniques that I have included in the second half of this book will be of interest and save you the time and research to discover the quickest and easiest way to achieve that authentic look, leaving you the enjoyment of your sewing in the knowledge that it will not only have a professional look but also provide your doll with a dress or outfit individually tailormade for her alone.

1

MEASURING YOUR DOLL

MEASURING YOUR DOLL

"Will it fit my doll"? is often the first question that comes to mind when confronted with a pattern to make clothes for a doll.

Most patterns are identified by the head-to-toe measurement of the doll for which they are designed to fit and whilst the height of a doll should determine that the length of the garment will be satisfactory, many of the other measurements about a doll's body can vary greatly. The width across the front and back chest between the armholes or around the upper chest can be too big or too little, and the waist too large or too small or even 'difficult to find'. Arms can come in different lengths and widths for the same height of doll. The upper arm can be quite plump and the wrist well defined whereas on a slimmer doll the arms can be thin and straight. The handspan, the width of the spread from thumb to little finger, is an important measurement. You can imagine the disappointment if, after all the effort in making up the garment, the doll cannot be dressed because the sleeve will not pass beyond the hand.

Legs too can vary in length and width and the upper and lower limbs can differ in proportion from one doll to another. Like the handspan, the width and length of a foot is important to ensure that the width of a trouser leg or fitted drawers is sufficient to be able to dress the doll afterwards. For bent limb dolls you will notice that the inner leg measurement from crutch to knee is shorter than the curved outer measurement

from hip to knee and this again has to be taken into consideration for underwear and trousers. The skirt for a bent limb doll which remains more permanently in a sitting position will need a shorter length as compared with a straight limbed doll which may remain upright supported by a doll stand, even though the body measurements may be similar.

Soft bodied dolls with their arms sewn to the main body and often under a shoulder plate need special attention to determine where the shoulder line finishes and the armhole begins. Also where the lower arms are made in porcelain or bisque, a shorter sleeve may be desired to show off the workmanship of a delicate wrist and an expressive hand.

To ensure that the pattern you select will be a good fit and reward your efforts, take the main measurements of your doll before you begin. Use the Measurement Chart on page 3 locating each measurement on the outline diagram of an average doll given beside it. Also read the accompanying notes detailing important measurements and construction areas which are significant when checking pattern pieces for size.

If you have more than one doll to dress, transfer the letter references onto separate sheets and keep an individual record for each doll. Luckily one 'fitting' session will be sufficient for the doll's entire wardrobe since, unlike people, dolls keep their trim or

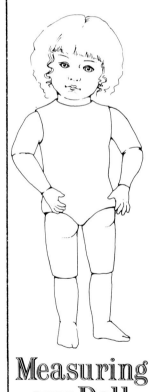

Measuring your Doll

MEASURING YOUR DOLL - continued

plump or short or long outlines no matter what their age! Perhaps you already keep a Doll Record of the main events and history of your doll - here would be a good place to include these measurements and any unusual features to remind you of particular problem areas.

Having taken these detailed measurements - what then?

Measure the pattern pieces and taking into account the additional seam allowances, compare these with the doll's measurements you have recorded to find out where you may need to alter the pattern before you cut your material. This is especially important if you will be using a precious piece of antique fabric which could be spoilt if incorrectly cut. If the two measurements are the same, bearing in mind also how much ease you may need in the width to be able to dress your doll afterwards, or if there is only up to a quarter inch difference, then the garment made up with those pattern pieces should be successful. However, if it is apparent that some alteration is needed then there are various ways of changing the pattern pieces to achieve a good fit.

All these various ways are explained in detail in Chapter 2.

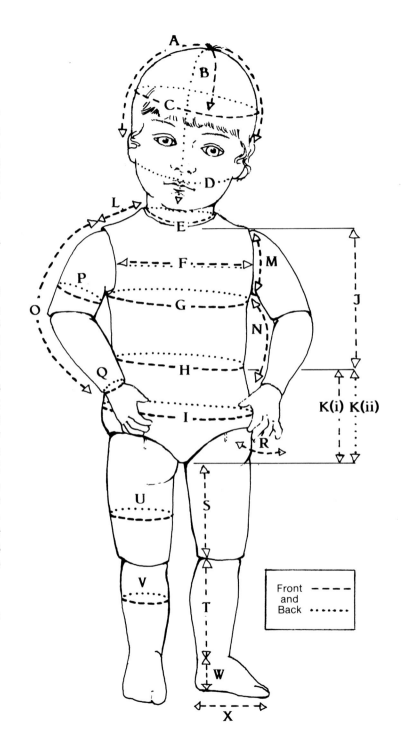

Name of Doll _____

Total Height _____

MEASUREMENT CHART

(For awkward small measurements, use cotton tape or string and transfer to a tape measure)

Inches
or
Cent'm

Head (over wig)

A.	From ear to ear over front hairline	_____
B.	Centre front (hairline) to nape of neck	_____
C.	Around head	_____
D.	From ear to ear across back of neck	_____

Body

E.	Around neck	_____
F.	Width across chest (front) between armholes (back)	_____ _____
G.	Around chest (underarm)	_____
H.	Around waist	_____
I.	Around hips	_____
J.	Centre neck to waist (front)	_____
K(i)	Centre waist to crutch (front)	_____
K(ii)	Centre waist to crutch (back)	_____

Inches
or
Cent'm

L.	Shoulder - neck to armhole	_____
M.	Armhole (half) - shoulder to side seam	_____

Arms and Hands

N.	Inside arm - armhole to wrist	_____
O.	Outside arm - shoulder to wrist	_____
P.	Around upper arm	_____
Q.	Around wrist	_____
R.	Handspan - thumb to little finger	_____

Legs and Feet

S.	Inside leg - crutch to knee	_____
T.	Lower leg - knee to ankle	_____
U.	Around leg - thigh	_____
V.	Around leg - calf	_____
W.	Ankle to floor	_____
X.	Foot - length of sole	_____

Overall lengths

Centre neck to knee	_____
Shoulder to ankle	_____
Waist to knee	_____

Measuring your Doll

MEASURING YOUR DOLL - continued

There are various areas during the construction of dolls clothes where the measurements outlined in the Measurement Chart are significant. These areas are listed individually under each reference number and heading for easy identification. Please remember that, when making outer garments for your doll, the thickness of the layers of underwear being worn will affect some of the measurements and any final measurement should be adjusted accordingly.

A.   From ear to ear over front hairline
- Exact for close fitting hats and bonnets
- Multiply by 2 or 2½ for a frill around the front of a hat or bonnet
- Multiply by 3 for a pleated edge around the front of a hat or bonnet
- Multiply by 1½ for the ruched crown of a hat
- Multiply by 1½ for the diameter of the circle for a mob cap or beret

B.   Centre front (hairline) to nape of neck
- Exact for close fitting hats and bonnets
- Multiply by 1½ for a fuller crown - exact for the lining
- Split measurement between crown and back crown depth when a hat or bonnet is formed by two sections

C.   Around head
- Exact for the headband of a beret

- Multiply by 2 for the circumference of a circle for a mob cap and even more if a deep outer frill is required

D.   From ear to ear across back of neck
- Exact for a close fitting hat or hat lining where the outer fabric is to be ruched, gathered or pleated
- Multiply by 2 for a bonnet neck frill
- Multiply by 3 for a bonnet neck pleating

E.   Around neck
- Exact for all garments with a close fitted neckline
- Add any extra measurement needed for the overlap of facing for a front or back opening of bodice
- Take note of the depth of the front scoop from shoulder to centre front and the width of back between shoulders. (Half this measurement is not necessarily where the shoulder seams should lie)

F.   Width across chest between armholes (front) and (back)
The whole proportion of the doll's body will be enhanced when a bodice or jacket fits this area correctly. The garment will hang evenly and the line of the armhole will follow the natural curve of the armsocket or joint.

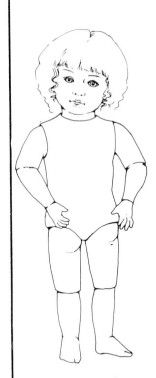

Measuring your Doll

MEASURING YOUR DOLL - continued

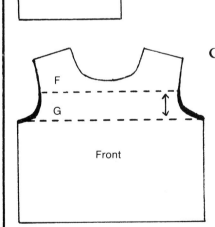

Back

Front

- Exact for a fitted bodice or jacket, taking into consideration turnings for facings. Note any difference between front and back measurements.
- Exact for a bodice lining to hold any fullness in the outer bodice
  Include extra measurement needed for tucks or ruched fullness.
- Multiply by 2 or 2½ for skirt fabric width to be gathered into a high yoke *
- Multiply by 3 for skirt fabric width to be pleated into a high yoke *
- * (Note: Add extra measurement for flat area needed at sides around lower armhole)

G. Around chest (underarm)
- Exact for waisted or high waisted bodice, allowing for opening facings
- Exact for bodice lining to hold any fullness of outer bodice.
- Exact for the shape of a princess line garment, or shaped bodice or jacket
- Multiply by 2 or 2½ for skirt to be gathered into a high waisted bodice
- Multiply by 3 for a similar pleated skirt
- This measurement, in relation to (**F**) above, will ensure the correct curve of the lower armhole to side seam (see diagram).

H. Around waist
- Exact for a waisted bodice, allowing for opening facings.
- Exact for waisted lining to hold any fullness of outer bodice.
- Exact for the shape of a princess line garment, or shaped bodice or jacket, especially when fashion dolls are being dressed.
  (Add up the width of panels being joined and subtract the total of the seam allowances as well as the overlap of facings).
- Multiply by 2 or 2½ for a gathered skirt fitted at true waistline.
- Multiply by 3 for a fully pleated skirt.
- Where spaced pleats are considered, multiply the number of pleats to be made by 3 and divide the remaining measurement equally by the number of pleats for the flat sections in between pleats.
- Multiply by 2 for a ribbon sash with a tied bow, and even more if a double bow is required.
- Exact for underwear plus the width of any facings.
- Exact for trouser waistband plus the width of any facings.
- For half-waistbands fastened at sides, measure front and back halves of waistline separately, especially where a doll has a more rounded stomach.

Measuring your Doll

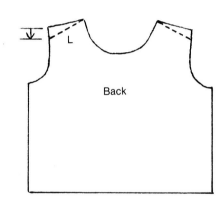

Back

L

I.   Around hips
- Add at least 2" (5 cm) for the fullness of underwear, drawers or combinations.
- Add up to 2" (5 cm) for extra fullness for the width of trousers
- Minimum lower bodice measurement for a low waisted dress style
- Minimum measurement for the lower edge of a longer jacket. More can be added depending on the shape to be achieved.
- Multiply by 2 for a ribbon sash on a low waisted dress, and even more if an important bow is required
- Multiply by $2\frac{1}{2}$ for skirt measurement to be gathered to a low waisted bodice.
- Multiply by 3 for skirt measurement to be pleated to a low waisted bodice.
- Multiply by 5 for skirt measurement to be double pleated to a low waisted bodice (see Notes on Pleats).

J.   Centre neck to waist
- For depth of bodice when skirt is added at true waist.
- Add up to 2" (5 cm) when outer bodice is bloused over lining, shaping or making tucks at side seam. Exact for lining measurement.

- Take into consideration with (K) for the depth of a low waisted bodice.
- Take into consideration with (part K) for the depth of a blouse or boy's shirt.

K(i)   Centre waist to crutch (front)
- For underwear drawers and combinations.
- For trousers, especially for bent limb dolls.
- For low waisted bodice, blouse or shirt length, see (J) above.

K(ii)   Centre waist to crutch (back)

- For underwear drawers and combinations.
- For trousers, add an extra 1" or 3 cm to ensure that doll will sit attractively, especially bent limb dolls.

L.   Shoulder - neck to armhole
- Exact for most garments.
- For backward slanting shoulder line: Take into consideration the depth from the true shoulder line to the point where the slanting shoulder meets the armhole to establish the angle of the backward slope (see diagram).

Measuring your Doll

M. **Armhole (half) - shoulder to side seam**
- Refer to diagram (**G**) showing lower curve of armhole. The depth of the armhole needs to be considered in relation to the construction of the bodice and width of the sleeve to allow flexibility when the doll is being dressed. The weight of the fabric being used should also be considered.

N. **Inside arm - armhole to wrist**
- To be considered in relation to the depth of armhole so that the finished sleeve will not fall beyond the desired length to elbow or wrist.
- For single piece sleeves, this measurement will follow the underarm seam.
- For two-part coat style sleeves, this measurement will follow the vertical centre of the undersleeve.

O. **Outside arm - shoulder to wrist**
- To be considered so that there is enough depth and fullness at top of sleeve, and more especially for two-part coat style sleeves, to allow arm movement as some dolls have an exaggerated arm socket and thick top arm.

P. **Around upper arm**
- To be considered to ensure that the sleeve width will be sufficient to allow the sleeve to fall gracefully over the arm.

- Multiply by $1\frac{1}{2}$ for fuller sleeves, and even more if an exaggerated oversleeve is required.

Q. **Around wrist**
- Exact for two-part coat or fitted sleeves with a side opening.
- Multiply by $1\frac{1}{2}$ for shirt sleeves fitted into a cuff.
- Multiply by 2 or more if an exaggerated frilled sleeve edge is required.
- To be taken into consideration with (**R**) for the lower edge of a sleeve or cuff.

R. **Handspan - thumb to little finger**
- Important: to be taken into consideration when calculating the measurement of the lower edge of a sleeve or cuff to ensure that neither is too tight to pass over the hand.

S. **Inside leg - crutch to knee**
- For underwear drawers and combinations.
- Add up to 2" (5 cm) as necessary if lower legs are to be gathered into leg bands.
- For trousers - front and back measurements may need to be considered separately for bent limb dolls.

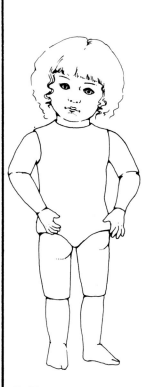

Measuring your Doll

T. Lower leg - knee to ankle
- The proportion of (**S**) and (**T**) measurements should be considered when deciding the length of a finished garment.
- The addition of (**S**) and (**T**) will ensure the correct length of long trousers.
- Exact or partial measurement will decide the length of socks.

U. Around leg - thigh
- Add up to 2" (5 cm) as necessary to ensure fullness of underwear drawers and combinations.

V. Around leg - calf
- Minimum width for underwear drawers and combinations legbands.
- Minimum width for legbands of trousers. (Take into consideration also (**X**) to ensure that legbands will not be too tight to pass over the foot).
- Exact for the width of socks allowing for elasticity of fabric. (Socks can then be pulled up full length)

W. Ankle to floor
- For the instep of socks to allow enough depth to prevent pulling or wrinkling at the ankles.
- For the depth of shoes.

X. Foot - length of sole
- Exact for socks to ensure easy fitting of shoe.

- Exact for shoes after taking into consideration the thickness of socks.

Overall Lengths

Centre neck to knee

To be considered to establish the overall length of a finished garment, especially when extra detail such as a plastron or revers, is added at centre front. When any alteration is made to the length of a garment, the proportion of a plastron or revers should also be altered. Also to decide how much longer you wish the finished garment to be below the knee.

Shoulder to ankle

For full length fashion dresses, again to establish the overall view, especially when any alterations to the proportion of a bodice or skirt are made.

Waist to knee (outer edge)

Useful for underwear drawers and combinations.

Essential for trousers, especially for bent limb dolls when the centre front and back measurements to crutch can differ from the curve of the outer body.

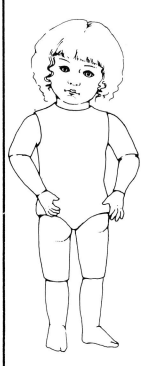

Measuring your Doll

2

ALTERING YOUR PATTERN

ALTERING YOUR PATTERN

GENERAL NOTES

Study the pattern pieces of the garment you wish to make and read the making-up instructions so as to gain an understanding of the various areas of construction. Make a note of any variation to the general seam allowance or complexity of style where extra attention may be needed when making the alterations you have identified, as you may not wish to change the overall design in any great detail.

The following pages explain in detail how the pattern pieces can be changed and are in the form of Questions with the Answers supported by diagrammatical illustrations.

These are divided into the various areas of construction of a garment, i.e. bodice or jacket, sleeve, collar, skirt, trousers etc., where there are Questions for altering your pattern 'if it is too big' and following on with the same sequence of Questions 'if your pattern is too small'. Also the various areas of measurement link up with those listed in the Measurement Chart so that you can trace the particular area you have identified where your pattern does not match your doll's measurements.

It may be that there is a combination of areas that need alteration. Read the answers for each area that is affected and combine the suggestions as altering one area may contribute towards part of the alteration needed nearby.

The suggestions for alteration in the "too big" answers are straight forward reductions of width or length whereas the suggestions for alteration in the "too small" answers are listed as "before" and "after". You will then be able to enlarge the pattern piece before assembling the mock-up which, if made up from the original size of the pattern pieces would be difficult to fit on your doll. The "after" notes give further suggestions for alteration while you have the mock-up fitted on your doll.

Preparing a Mock-up for Fitting

So that you can keep the original pattern intact, trace the outlines of the pattern pieces onto kitchen roll or tissue paper, old sheeting or fine vylene, following any special cutting out instruction. (Kitchen roll paper sheets can be joined with sticky tape for larger pattern pieces.) Use a soft 2B pencil to draw in all the pattern markings, seam lines as well as vertical centre and facing lines.

You can use the copy pattern to make up a "mock-up" of the garment to try on the doll and adjust the pattern where you have identified the need.

It will be easier to fit the mock-up on the doll in sections rather than join all the seams together and try it on as a complete unit.

Altering your Pattern

ALTERING YOUR PATTERN - continued

Notes on the construction of your mock-up are given in the beginning of each section on the following pages. The mock-up can either be pinned or tacked together along the marked seam lines. While it is easier to take out and re-insert pins when making an alteration, you may prefer to tack with tacking thread if there is any likelihood of the doll's face or body being scratched by the pins when trying-on or altering the mock-up. A fresh not-too-thick sewing needle with a sharp point is essential when tacking paper or tissue together. However, for continuity I refer to the use of pins to join the seams but use whichever method you prefer.

Any curved seam allowance - around neck or lower armhole - should be snipped to allow the seam to lie flat around the doll's body, and you will find it easier to adjust the pattern and move pins if the mock-up is tried on your doll with the right side against your doll's body.

AFTER ALTERATION

When you have completed all the alterations, take a red or blue coloured soft pencil and draw over the pins or tacking thread to mark any new seam lines, vertical centre and fold lines to distinguish them from the original markings. Carefully unpin the mock-up and make a new master pattern where necessary using paper or thin card. Transfer all the markings and revised construction lines onto the new master pattern. Also remember to identify each pattern piece such as "bodice front" or "side back" and draw in the arrowed line for the straight of fabric. Record on each pattern piece the name or make of the doll for which the pattern has been created. This is especially important if you are dressing several dolls of differing proportions with the same basic style.

Key to Symbols on Illustrations in this book

↑↓ Arrow indicates where to measure for correct measurement required.

↑↓↑↓ Several arrows in a line. Adding these together gives correct measurement required.

▨ Areas to cut away to make pattern smaller.

▦ Areas where extra tissue is added to make pattern larger.

W/S Wrong side of fabric.

R/S Right side of fabric.

C/F Centre front.

C/B Centre back.

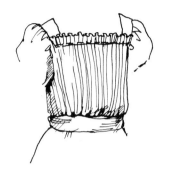

Bodice or Jacket

ALTERING A BODICE OR JACKET

IF PATTERN IS TOO BIG

Construction of Mock-up - Pin shoulders and side seam, as well as any other vertical seam if applicable. Where there is a ruched or pleated panel in the bodice, use the equivalent lining section for the mock-up. Turn back any facings. Snip neck and lower armhole curves within seam allowance.

Arrange pin tucks or pleats, or run a gathering thread where necessary.

Try on mock-up with right sides against the doll's body so that any seam can be adjusted easily.

The following Pattern Alteration Notes are in the form of Questions and Answers. Select the particular problem area and try out the suggested alterations.

PATTERN ALTERATION

Too wide across front or back chest between armholes and around front or back neck when centre is against a fold?

Keeping shoulder and side seams even with doll's outline pin a dart from neck down centre, tapering towards lower edge until fullness has been taken up. This will realign the centre fold of pattern. Re-draw neck seamline following doll's neck curve.

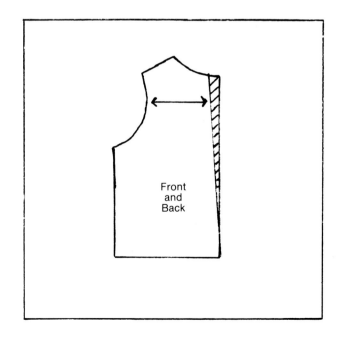

Front and Back

IF PATTERN IS TOO BIG

PATTERN ALTERATION - continued

Too wide across front or back chest between armholes and around front or back neck when pattern has a front or back opening?

Keeping shoulder and armhole seamline even with doll's outline re-fold facings and mark new fold line. Realign new vertical centre line of bodice. Trim away excess facings, re-draw neck seam following doll's neck curve.

Too wide across front and back chest between armholes and around neck for shaped panelled bodice?

Keeping shoulder and armhole seamline even with doll's outline re-pin the shaped seams and/or turn wider facings at opening to reduce fullness evenly, keeping in mind the proportion of the bodice design.

Only if further reduction of the width is required should you consider taking a tuck down the centre fold.

Should this latter alteration be on a lining panel, remember to make an alteration to the top ruched or pleated layer. This, however, may not be necessary if the extra fullness can be incorporated with added effect bringing gathers closer together or pleats further overlapped at top and bottom but keeping side edges even with lining.

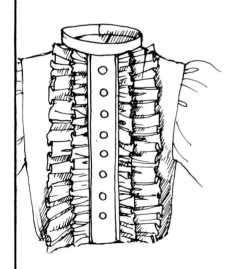

Bodice or Jacket

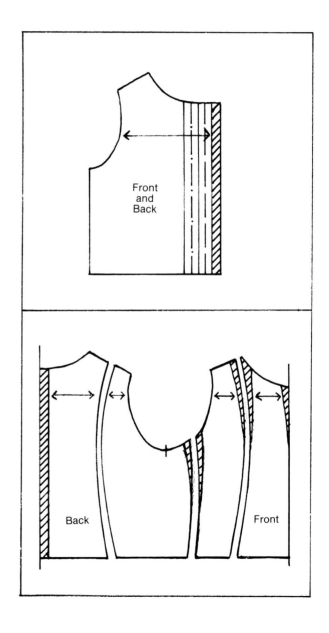

Front and Back

Back   Front

PATTERN ALTERATION continued

Too wide across shoulders?

Mark pattern where doll's arm meets body at shoulder line. Keeping neck edge of shoulder correct, re-draw armhole seamline from new marking tapering down towards armhole curve.

Too wide across front chest and shoulders?

Adjust as for Shoulders but continue to re-draw armhole seamline around armhole curve to side seamline.

Too deep at armhole?

There are two alternatives:

a) When the shoulder and the centre front depth and width are correct, the armhole curve will need to be built up from the side seam. Measure amount needed, take off mock-up and add extra tissue or fabric securing it with pins or sticky tape. Try on again and re-draw armhole seamline following the doll's outline.

b) When the depth of the side seam and the overall width are both correct, re-pin shoulder seam tapering from armhole to neck edge.

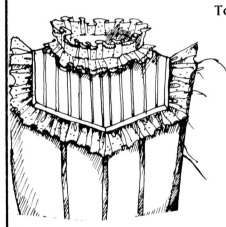

Bodice or Jacket

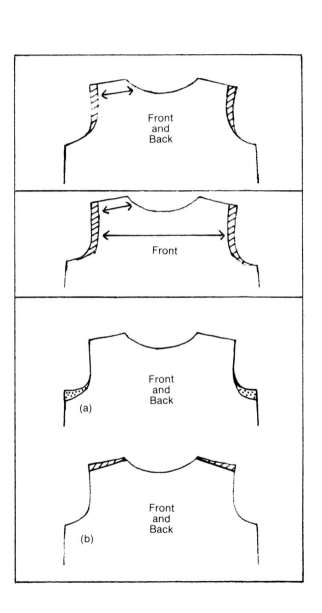

Bodice or Jacket

PATTERN ALTERATION continued

Special Notes

The depth and curve of the armhole should always be considered in relation to:

a)   the complexity of garment so as to dress the doll with ease when finished.

b)   the degree of stiffness of fabric being used for flexibility of arm movement.

c)   The fullness of sleeve head to produce a pleasing outline and allow the sleeve to hang naturally.

Too big around chest at underarm?

Re-pin side seam tapering from armhole down to lower edge.

Too big around waist?

Re-pin side seam tapering from lower edge towards armhole.

Too big around hips? (for low waisted bodice, long jacket or princess style panels)

Re-pin side seam tapering from lower edge towards waist or reduce fullness evenly across shaped panels.

(Remember to allow for fullness of any underwear or the bulkiness of trousers as too much reduction can restrict the flare of a low skirt or a long jacket.)

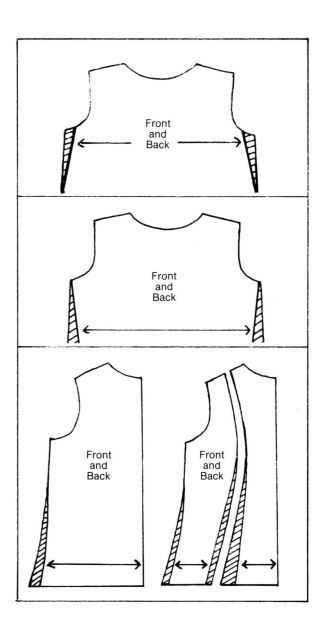

IF PATTERN IS TOO BIG

PATTERN ALTERATION continued

Too long from neck to waist?

> Bearing in mind the overall effect, pin a tuck around chest or cut off required depth from lower edge at waistline.

Too long from neck to hips? (for a low waisted bodice, long jacket or princess style panels)

> Bearing in mind the overall effect, pin a tuck either at chest or waist level, or cut off required depth from lower edge at hipline.

Bodice or Jacket

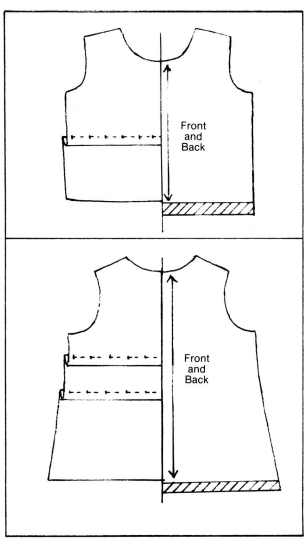

IF PATTERN IS TOO SMALL

Construction of Mock-up - When the pattern piece appears to be too small, it is likely that an assembled mock-up of the bodice or jacket will not fit around the doll's body. Therefore, some alteration will need to be carried out before pinning the pattern pieces together. The Pattern Alteration Notes in this Section are headed "before" and "after" and give instructions for any adjustments to be made before the mock-up is assembled, followed by further adjustments that may be necessary after the mock-up has been tried on the doll. See also the Construction Notes at the beginning of Section 1.

PATTERN ALTERATION

Too narrow across front or back chest between armholes and around front or back neck when centre is against a fold?

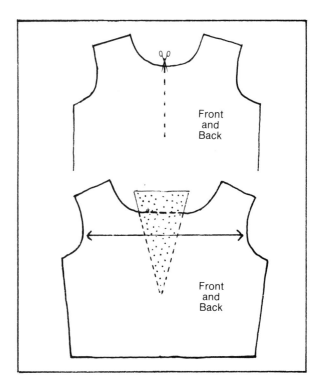

Front and Back

Front and Back

Before

Cut down centre line from neck edge and open out to required width. Pin a strip of tissue to fit gap and extend over neck edge.

After

Adjust added tissue as necessary. Realign centre line. Re-draw neck seamline following doll's neck curve.

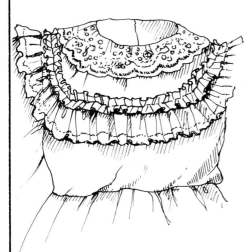

Bodice or Jacket

IF PATTERN IS TOO SMALL

PATTERN ALTERATION continued

Too narrow across front or back chest between armholes and around front or back neck when pattern has a front or back opening?

Before

Add strip of tissue to opening edges.

After

Refold facings. Re-draw fold line and vertical centre line. Re-draw neck seamline following doll's neck curve.

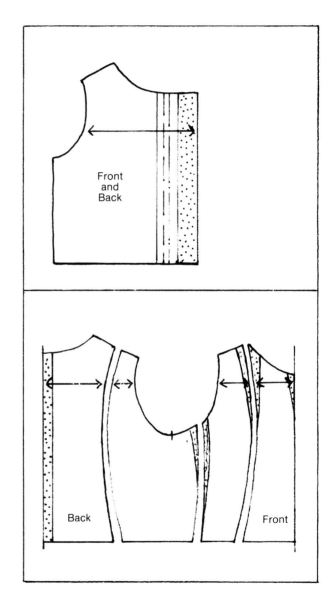

Front and Back

Back   Front

Too narrow across front and back chest between armholes and around neck for shaped panelled bodice?

Before

Add a strip of tissue to opening edges, and down each vertical shaped seam to increase overall width to required amount.

After

Adjust and re-pin any seams where you have been too generous in adding extra tissue. Check fold line of facings. Realign vertical centre line. Re-draw neck seamline following doll's neck curve.

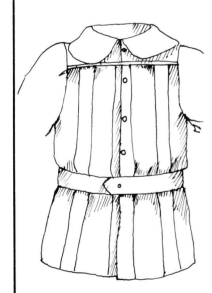

Bodice or Jacket

IF PATTERN IS TOO SMALL

<u>PATTERN ALTERATION</u> continued

Too narrow across shoulders

<u>Before</u>

Add extra tissue to front and back armhole edge from lower curve to shoulder edge.

<u>After</u>

Mark pattern where doll's arm meets body at shoulder line.
Keeping neck edge of shoulder correct, re-draw armhole seamline from new shoulder marking tapering down towards lower armhole curve.

Too narrow across front chest and shoulders?

<u>Before</u>

Add extra tissue to front armhole edge from shoulder to underarm.

<u>After</u>

Mark pattern where doll's arm meets body at shoulder line.
Keeping neck edge of shoulder correct, re-draw armhole seamline from new shoulder marking to side seamline.

Taper back shoulder to match new width of front shoulder.

Bodice
or Jacket

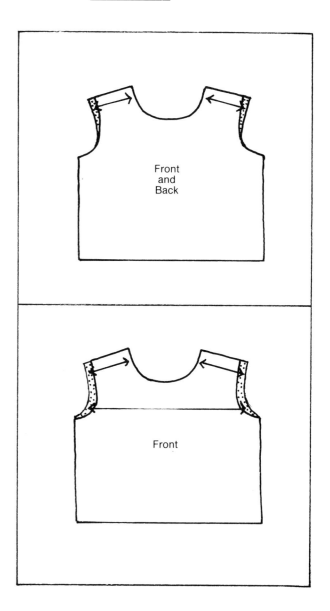

IF PATTERN IS TOO SMALL

PATTERN ALTERATION continued

Too shallow at armhole?

Before

Add extra tissue to shoulder edges. Leave a small section of side seam at underarm unpinned.

After

There are two alternatives:

a) Keeping the shoulder and the depth and width of bodice correct, re-draw the armhole seamline following the doll's outline. Trim away excess at lower curve of armhole to allow pattern to lie flat against doll's body.

b) When the depth of the side seam and the overall width are correct, re-pin shoulder seamline tapering from armhole to neck edge.

Special Notes on Armhole Shape

The depth and curve of the armhole should always be considered in relation to:

i) the complexity of garment so as to dress the doll with ease when finished.

ii) the degree of stiffness of fabric being used for flexibility of arm movement.

iii) the fullness of sleeve head to produce a pleasing outline and allow the sleeve to hang naturally.

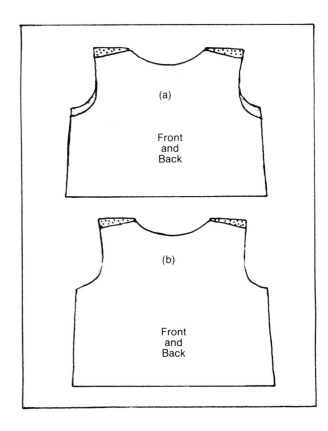

(a) Front and Back

(b) Front and Back

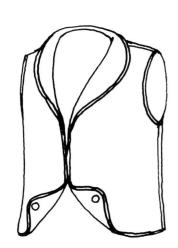

Bodice or Jacket

IF PATTERN IS TOO SMALL

PATTERN ALTERATION continued

Too small around chest at underarm?

Before

Add extra tissue to side edges.

After

Adjust and re-pin side seamlines tapering from armhole to lower edge.

Too small around waist?

Before

Add extra tissue to side edges.

After

Adjust and re-pin side seamlines tapering from lower edge towards armhole.

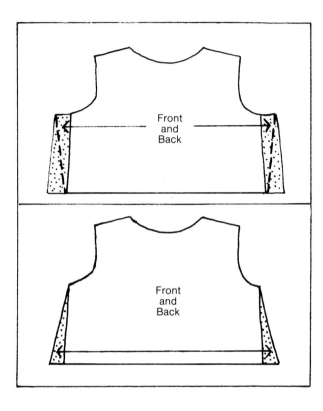

Bodice or Jacket

IF PATTERN IS TOO SMALL

PATTERN ALTERATION continued

Too small around hips? (for low waisted bodice, long jacket or princess style panels)

Before

Add extra tissue to side and any vertical shaped edge as well as opening edges tapering from waist to lower edge.

After

Adjust and re-pin side seamlines tapering from waist towards lower edge, or adjust and re-pin shaped panels or opening edges where you have been too generous in adding extra tissue.

(Remember to allow for fullness of any underwear or the bulkiness of trousers so as not to restrict the flare of a low skirt or a long jacket.)

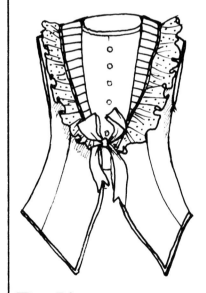

Bodice or Jacket

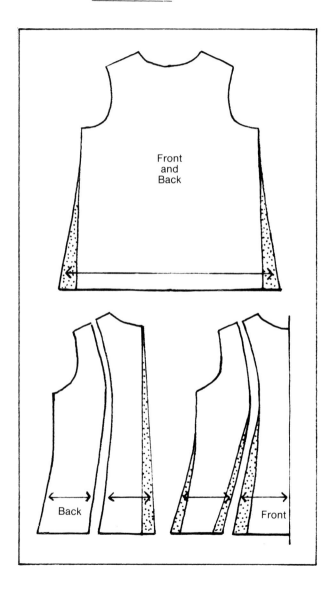

IF PATTERN IS TOO SMALL

PATTERN ALTERATION continued

Too short from neck to waist?

Before

Decide where extra depth is required either above or below armhole level. Add a strip of tissue either across upper chest between armholes or to lower edge of bodice as required.

After

Adjust and re-pin added tissue as necessary, and/or trim lower edge to required depth.

Too short from neck to hips? (for low waisted bodice, long jacket or princess style panels)

Before

Decide where extra depth is required either above or below armhole level and/or at lower edge.

Add a strip of tissue across upper chest, at waist level or at lower edge as required.

After

Adjust and re-pin added tissue as necessary at chest or waist and/or trim lower edge to required depth.

Bodice or Jacket

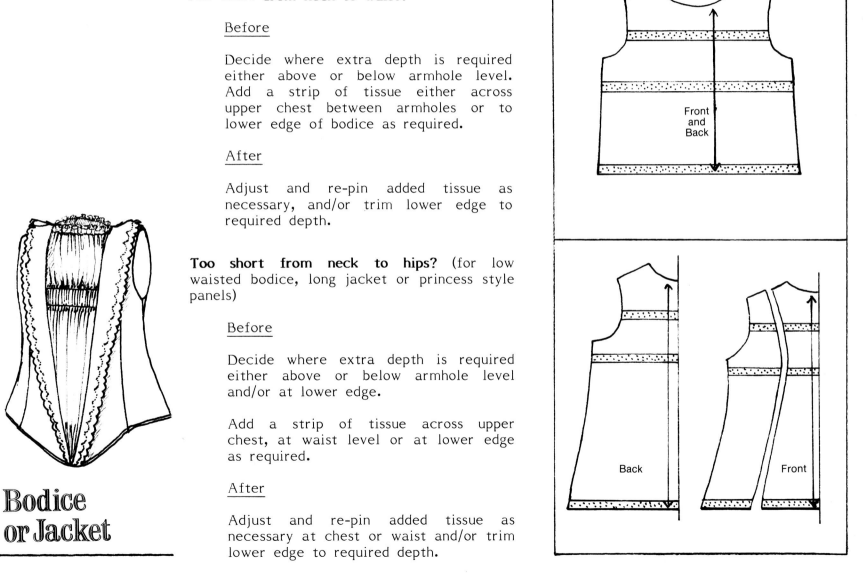

Front and Back

Back

Front

IF PATTERN IS TOO BIG

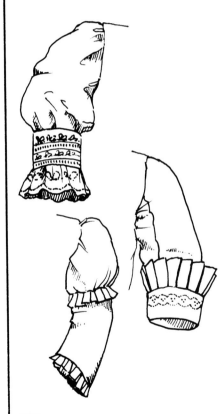

Construction of Mock-up - Make any adjustments to one sleeve only, as two sleeves are always cut from an identical pattern piece.

For a one-piece sleeve, run a gathering thread or make tucks around sleeve head as applicable. If lower edge of sleeve is gathered or pleated into a cuff, pin cuff to sleeve now. Pin underarm seam. (See Special Note below.)

For a two-piece or coat style sleeve, pin back seam of top sleeve to undersleeve. Run a gathering thread around sleeve head so that any fullness or ease can be drawn in when fitting sleeve to bodice. Pin inner seam. (See Special Note below.)

For a sleeve with an elaborate oversleeve, cut out both oversleeve and sleeve lining for the mock-up. Use the sleeve lining which can be in the shape of a one-piece or coat style sleeve and follow above instruction as applicable. The fullness of the oversleeve can be adjusted separately in relation to any adjustment made to the sleeve lining.

Continue for any of the above sleeve shapes -

Draw up gathering thread to distribute fullness or ease around sleeve head, or re-adjust tucks to fit armhole of bodice. Pin sleeve head in place. Clip curve at lower armhole. Try on bodice and sleeve with right sides against the doll's body so that the sleeve width and length can be adjusted more easily.

Special Note:

Before closing underarm or inner seam of sleeve ready to fit to mock-up bodice, check the sleeve length from centre top of sleeve head to wrist as well as the width around upper and lower sleeve and compare these with the corresponding measurements you have recorded of your doll's arm. Identify where you feel an alteration is needed, bearing in mind the desired effect of the finished sleeve for length and fullness.

Sleeve

IF PATTERN IS TOO BIG

PATTERN ALTERATION

Too wide around upper and lower arm?

Bearing in mind the desired effect of fullness, pin a tuck down centre length from sleeve head to wrist.

This alteration may cause the top section of a coat sleeve to be out of proportion with the undersection. So alternatively re-pin the inner and outer seamlines to reduce fullness evenly.

Too wide around upper arm only?

(a) re-pin underarm seamline from armhole to elbow.

or(b) pin a dart from sleeve head tapering down to elbow.

or for coat sleeve, re-pin inner and outer seamlines from armhole to elbow to reduce fullness evenly.

Sleeve

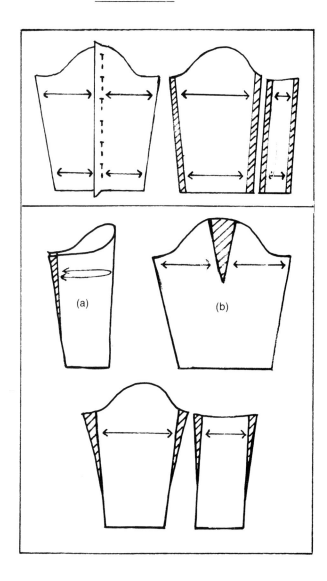

IF PATTERN IS TOO BIG

PATTERN ALTERATION - continued

Too wide around lower arm and wrist?

Firstly, the minimum width of the lower edge of a sleeve finishing at the wrist should be at least twice the width of the doll's handspan to ensure ease of dressing.

Make any reduction necessary by -

For one piece sleeve,

Either (a)
    re-pin underarm seamline from elbow to wrist.

or(b) pin a dart at centre outer edge from wrist tapering upwards until fullness has been reduced.

For coat sleeve, re-pin inner and outer seamlines from wrist upwards to reduce fullness evenly.

Too long at outer arm, from centre top of sleeve head to wrist?

Take a horizontal tuck in sleeve head to match any reduction already carried out on the bodice armhole.

Check that reduction does not make the curve of the sleeve head too abrupt, especially where it fits into the back bodice armhole.

Sleeve

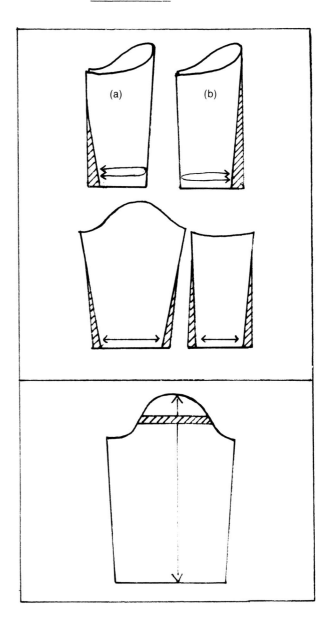

IF PATTERN IS TOO BIG

PATTERN ALTERATION - continued

Too long at inside arm from armhole to wrist?

If the centre sleeve measurement is exact:

(a) Take a dart from inside seam towards centre of sleeve at elbow.

(b) Reduce lower edge at wrist tapering from centre to underarm seam.

Cuff

When making any alterations to the length of a sleeve which has an attached cuff, the depth of the cuff should be taken into consideration, and also adjusted if necessary.

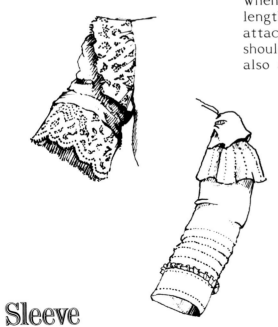

Sleeve

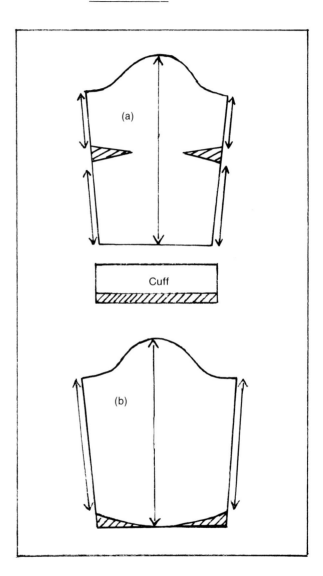

(a)

Cuff

(b)

IF PATTERN IS TOO SMALL

Construction of Mock-up - Make any adjustments to one sleeve only, as two sleeves are always cut from an identical pattern piece.

When the pattern piece appears to be too small, it is likely that an assembled mock-up of the sleeve will not fit over the doll's arm, therefore some alteration will need to be carried out before pinning the pattern to the bodice section.

The following notes are headed 'before' and 'after' and give instructions for any adjustments to be made <u>before</u> the mock-up is assembled, followed by further adjustments that may be necessary <u>after</u> the sleeve pattern has been pinned to the bodice.

(See also the Construction Notes given at the beginning of Section 1.)

PATTERN ALTERATION

Too narrow around upper and lower arm?

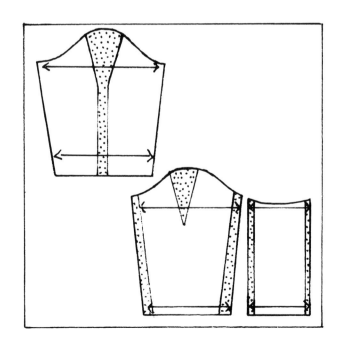

Before

For one piece sleeve, cut down centre from sleeve head to wrist and add a strip of tissue to required width.

For coat sleeve, add a strip of tissue to inner and outer edges of top and under sections. Check that sleeve head will be wide enough, otherwise cut down from centre of top sleeve and add tissue to required width.

After

Adjust and re-pin added tissue as necessary. Mark new seamlines.

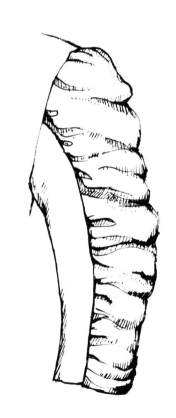

Sleeve

PATTERN ALTERATION - continued

Too narrow around upper arm only?

Before

For one piece sleeve,

Either (a)
Add a strip of tissue to underarm edges from armhole to elbow.

or(b) Cut down from centre of sleeve head to elbow and insert a strip of tissue to required width.

For coat sleeve, add a strip of tissue to inner and outer edges of top and under sections.

After

Adjust and re-pin added tissue as necessary. Mark new seamlines.

Sleeve

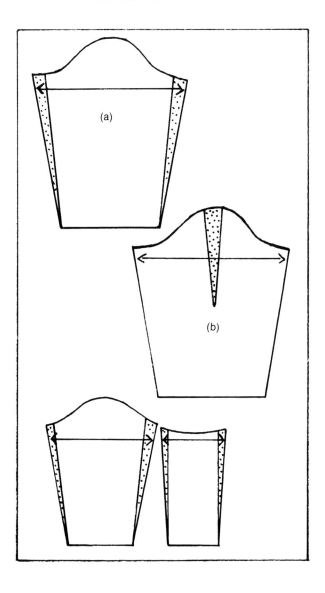

IF PATTERN IS TOO SMALL

PATTERN ALTERATION - continued

Too narrow around lower arm and wrist?

<u>Before</u>

For one piece sleeve,

Either (a)
    Add a strip of tissue to underarm edges from elbow to wrist.

or(b) Cut at centre from wrist to elbow and insert strip of tissue to required width.

    For coat sleeve, add a strip of tissue to inner and outer edges of top and under sections.

<u>After</u>

Adjust and re-pin added tissue as necessary. Mark new seamlines.

Remember that the minimum width of the lower edge of a sleeve finishing at the wrist should be at least twice the width of the doll's handspan to ensure ease of dressing.

Cuff

When making any alterations to the lower edge of a sleeve which has an attached cuff, the same adjustments should be transferred to the cuff.

Sleeve

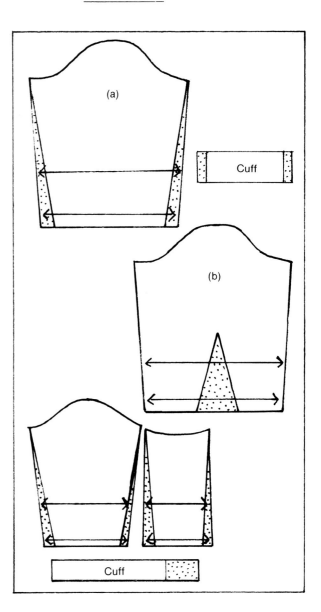

IF PATTERN IS TOO SMALL

PATTERN ALTERATION - continued

Too short at outer arm from centre top of sleevehead to wrist?

<u>Before</u>

Either (a)
   Cut sleeve horizontally across centre of sleevehead and add a strip of tissue to match any increase made to the bodice armhole.

or(b) If sleevehead is correct, cut sleeve horizontally at elbow and add a strip of tissue, tapering to each inner edge.

<u>After</u>

Adjust and re-pin added tissue as required.

Too short at inside arm from armhole to wrist?

<u>Before</u>

Either (a)
   Cut sleeve horizontally from inner edge to centre at elbow, and add a strip of tissue to form a dart.

or(b) Add a strip of tissue to lower edge to extend sleeve at wrist edge.

<u>After</u>

Adjust and re-pin added tissue as required.

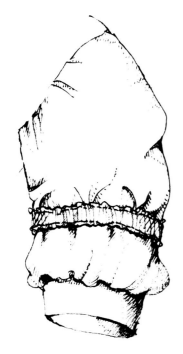

Sleeve

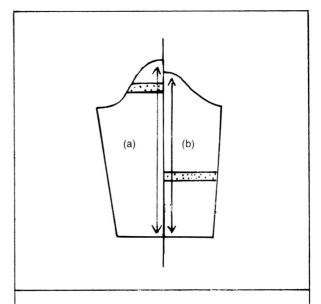

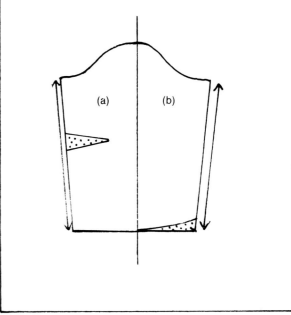

IF PATTERN IS TOO BIG

Construction of Mock-up - Make any adjustments to one collar piece only, as the top and undersection of a collar are always cut from an identical pattern piece.

Consider what alterations have been made around the neck of the bodice or jacket and make an equivalent subtraction to the collar so that it will fit the bodice neckline of the mock-up.

Pin collar to bodice or jacket and readjust any alterations to obtain a good fit. Try bodice on doll and check that the shape and the proportion of the amended collar is correct.

PATTERN ALTERATION

One piece collar with centre back placed on a fold - too large?

Pin a tuck at back fold equal to the amount of tuck or dart made at back bodice neckline. At each front edge cut away half the amount reduced at front bodice neckline.

(Check that collar centre back fold will lie along bodice centre back and front edges lie even with bodice centre front.) Mark new seamlines.

For a Peter Pan shaped collar

The neck curve should match the neck curve of bodice. Re-shape neck curve of collar as necessary. Mark new seamlines.

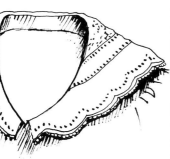

Collar or Revers

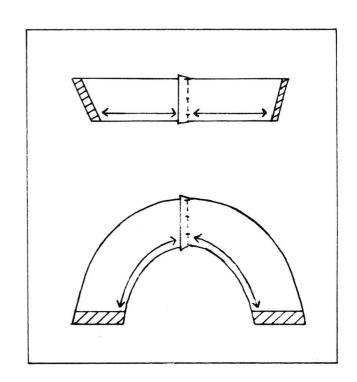

PATTERN ALTERATION - continued

Sailor Collar with long points - too wide and/or too long?

> Pin a tuck in collar to reduce fullness in relation to where and by how much the neck and front of bodice have been altered. Mark new seamlines.

Revers of a Jacket, or Decorative Revers on a Bodice - too large?

> Pin a tuck to reduce fullness in relation to where and by how much the front of jacket or bodice has been altered. Mark new seamlines.

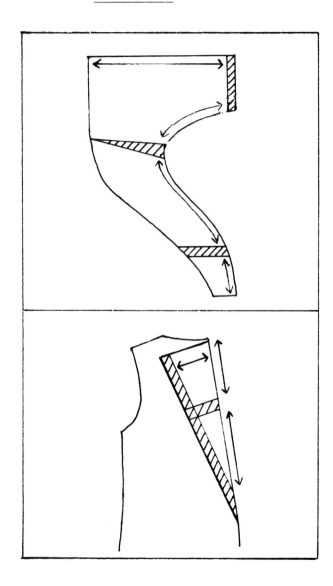

Collar or Revers

IF PATTERN IS TOO SMALL

Construction of Mock-up - Make any adjustments to one collar piece only, as the top and undersection of a collar are always cut from an identical pattern piece.

Consider what alterations have been made around the neck of the bodice or jacket and make an equivalent addition to the collar so that it will fit the bodice neckline of the mock-up.

Pin collar to bodice or jacket and readjust any alterations to obtain a good fit. Try bodice on doll and check that the shape and the proportion of the amended collar is correct.

PATTERN ALTERATION

One piece collar with centre back placed on a fold - too small?

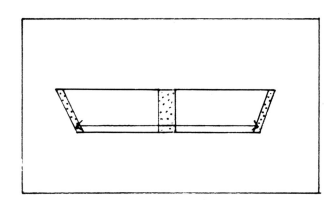

Before

Cut back fold and add a strip of tissue equal to the amount added to back bodice neckline. Add a strip of tissue to front edges equal to half the amount added to front bodice neckline.

After

Adjust and re-pin added tissue as necessary when adding collar to bodice.

(Check that collar centre back fold will lie along bodice centre back and front edges lie even with bodice centre front.) Mark new seamlines.

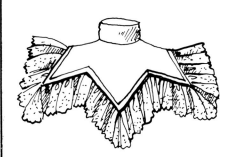

Collar or Revers

PATTERN ALTERATION - continued

For a Peter Pan shaped collar

The neck curve should match the neck curve of bodice. Re-shape neck curve of collar as necessary. Mark new seamlines.

Sailor Collar with long points - too narrow or too short?

Before

Cut back fold and add a strip of tissue equal to the amount added to back bodice neckline. Add extra tissue to front points in relation to where and by how much the front bodice has been altered.

After

Adjust and re-pin added tissue as necessary when attaching collar to bodice. Mark new seamlines.

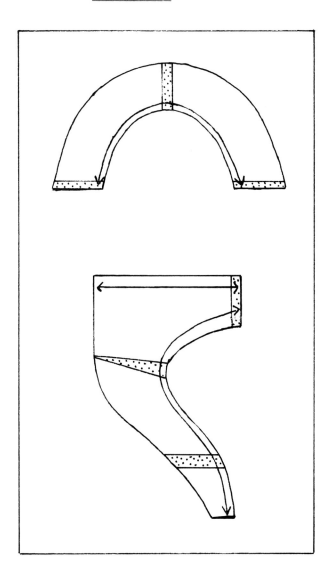

Collar or Revers

PATTERN ALTERATION - continued

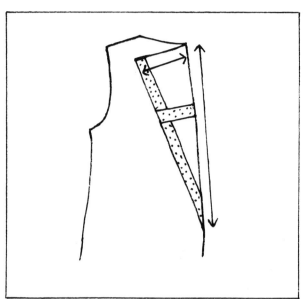

Revers of a Jacket, or Decorative Revers on a Bodice - too small?

Before

Cut and add extra tissue to width or length in relation to where and by how much the front of jacket or bodice has been altered.

After

Adjust and re-pin added tissue as necessary when attaching revers to jacket front or bodice. Mark new seamlines.

Collar or Revers

Skirt

ALTERING A SKIRT

IF PATTERN IS TOO BIG

Construction of Mock-up - Skirts for dolls clothes are generally constructed from a rectangle of fabric, either gathered or pleated to fit a bodice. Cut out the required rectangle and pin seam leaving opening as required. Run gathering line for gathers or form pleats as instructed.

For flared skirts, generally made up of several shaped panels, pin all seams, leaving opening as required.

Mark where a skirt is to be tucked horizontally or where added decoration is required; also mark hemline. Pin skirt to bodice and try on doll, still having the right side against the doll's body for ease of alteration.

PATTERN ALTERATION

Too wide around the waist?

Measure the total width of the lower edge of bodice to which the skirt is to be attached and recalculate the required width of the skirt rectangle, bearing in mind the thickness of the fabric.

Gathered skirt:

2 - $2\frac{1}{2}$ times waist measurement (3 or even 4 times for extra flimsy fabric)

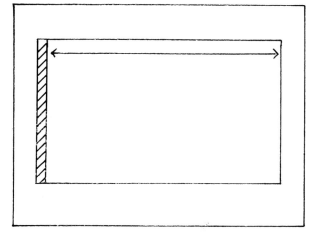

IF PATTERN IS TOO BIG

PATTERN ALTERATION - continued

Pleated skirt:

> 3 times waist measurement. N.B. If you wish to keep the fullness of the original skirt measurement, pleats can be further reduced by overlapping the folded edges. This can be especially effective for the back of the dress where a fuller effect may be required.

> (See Notes on Pleats and Gathers)

Flared skirt with panels

> Re-pin seams tapering from waist to hips.

Too wide around the hips?

> For a low waisted gathered or pleated skirt, measure the total width of the lower edge of bodice and recalculate the width of skirt rectangle. Follow the same instructions and basic calculations for adjusting skirt at waistline.

> For flared skirt with panels, re-pin seams tapering from hips to lower edge.

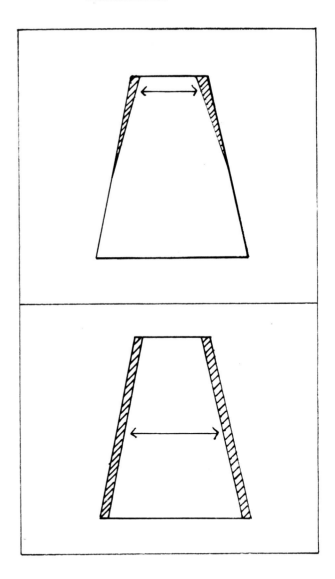

Skirt

IF PATTERN IS TOO BIG

PATTERN ALTERATION - continued

Too long from waist to knee or calf?

Decide on the required length of skirt. Cut off excess depth of skirt rectangle. Re-draw hemline and adjust any tucks or skirt decorations.

For flared skirt with panels, cut off excess depth at lower edge. Check flare of total skirt at lower edge is in proportion with the size of the doll.

Skirt

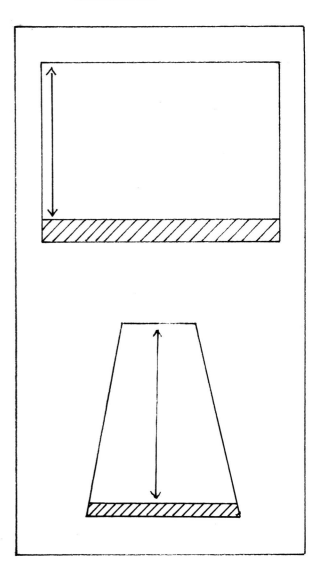

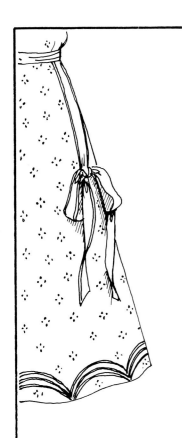

Skirt

IF PATTERN IS TOO SMALL

Construction of Mock-up - When the skirt rectangle appears to be too small, it is likely that an assembled mock-up will not fit over the doll. Therefore the majority of alterations will need to be carried out before pinning the pattern to the bodice section.

The notes under Section 2 are headed 'before' and 'after' and give instructions for any adjustments to be made <u>before</u> the mock-up is assembled followed by further adjustments that may be necessary <u>after</u> the skirt has been pinned to the bodice and tried on the doll. See also Construction Notes at the beginning of Section 1.

PATTERN ALTERATION

Too small around the waist?

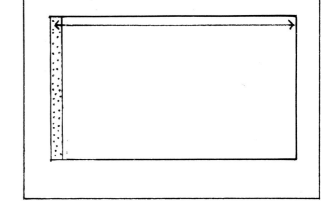

<u>Before</u>

Measure the total width of the lower edge of bodice to which the skirt is to be attached and recalculate the required width of the skirt rectangle bearing in mind the thickness of the fabric. Pin extra tissue to pattern rectangle as required.

Gathered Skirt:

2 - 2½ times waist measurement (3 or even 4 times for extra flimsy fabric).

Pleated Skirt:

3 times waist measurement.

<u>After</u>

Adjust and re-pin added tissue as necessary.

(See Notes on Pleats and Gathers)

IF PATTERN IS TOO SMALL

PATTERN ALTERATION - continued

Flared skirt with panels

Before

Add strips of tissue to as many edges of the panels as necessary to increase the overall measurement to fit the waist.

After

Adjust and re-pin added tissue as necessary tapering from waist to hips.

Too small around the hips?

For low waisted, gathered or pleated skirt.

Follow the same instructions and basic measurements for adjusting skirt at waistline.

Too short from waist to knee or calf?

Before

Decide on the required length of skirt and add extra tissue at lower edge.

After

Re-draw hemline and adjust any horizontal tucks or skirt decoration.

Skirt

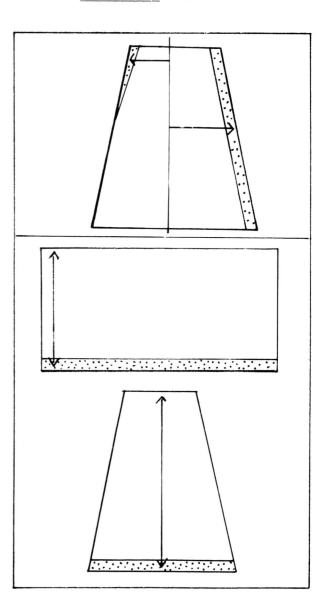

Trousers

IF PATTERN IS TOO BIG

<u>Construction of Mock-up</u> - Pin front, back and inside leg seams, leaving any openings free. Pin waistband and legbands as required, or turn under casings. Try on mock-up trousers with right sides against the doll's body so that any seam can be adjusted easily.

PATTERN ALTERATION

Too wide across front or back at waist?

(1)   Keeping centre front and back seams correct, take a dart from waist tapering towards hips at side edges.

If the trousers have side openings, taper the centre front and/or back seams from waist to hips. Remember to adjust waistband to fit new waist measurement.

(2)   If there is only a small difference and the back waist is gathered into a waistband, gathering in the excess fullness may be all that is necessary.

Too wide around hips?

Remember to allow plenty of fullness here so that the doll will be able to sit with ease. Especially important for bent limb dolls.

Make a dart at side edges, keeping front and back seams correct.

If trousers have a side opening adjust fullness at centre front or back seams or both.

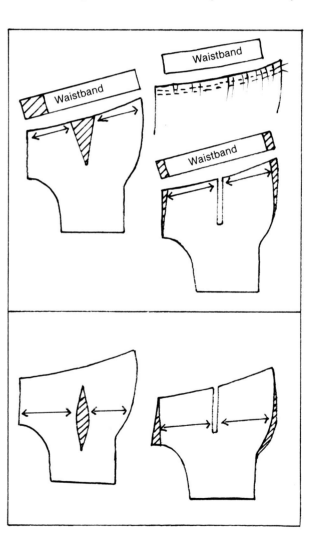

IF PATTERN IS TOO BIG

PATTERN ALTERATION - continued

Too wide around thigh?

Take a dart from lower edge of leg towards hips at side edge. May be incorporated with reduction over hips.

For bent limb dolls adjust inner leg seam, especially when front or back seams have been adjusted over hips.

If the reduction needed is minimal and the trouser legs are gathered into a legband, gathering in the excess fullness may be all that is necessary.

Please Note

Any reduction of the lower leg will need to be reflected in the leg band. Ensure that the final width of lower leg is sufficient for the trousers to pass over the doll's foot when being dressed.

Too long from waist to crutch?

Length can be reduced at the waist edge, or across the hips with a horizontal tuck.

Remember to keep enough ease in the back depth to allow the doll to sit.

Trousers

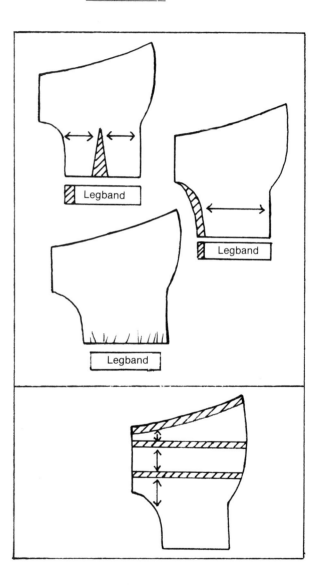

IF PATTERN IS TOO BIG

PATTERN ALTERATION - continued

Too long from crutch to knee?

Shorten length of the trouser leg at lower edge. Remember to check inside and outside leg measurements of bent limb dolls so that the doll can be dressed with ease.

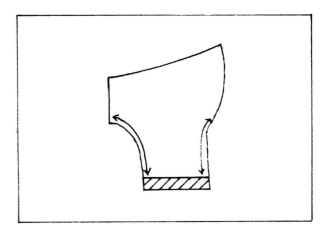

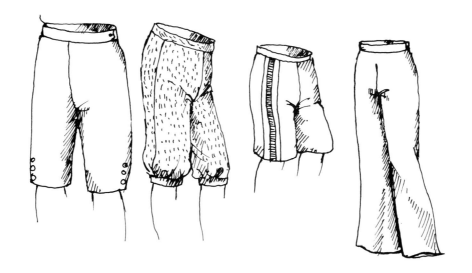

Trousers

IF PATTERN IS TOO SMALL

Construction of Mock-up - When the pattern pieces appear to be too small it is likely that an assembled mock-up will not fit over the doll. Therefore the majority of alterations will need to be carried out before pinning the pattern pieces together.

The notes under Section 2 are headed "before" and "after" and give instructions for any adjustments to be made <u>before</u> the mock-up is assembled, followed by any further adjustments that may be necessary <u>after</u> the mock-up has been tried on the doll's body.

After initial adjustment, pin front, back and inside leg seams, leaving any openings free. Pin waistband and legbands as required, or turn under casings. Try on mock-up trousers with right sides against doll's body so that any further alteration needed can be made more easily.

PATTERN ALTERATION

Too narrow across front or back at waist?

<u>Before</u>

Cut down side edge from waist and open out to required width. Pin a strip of tissue to fill gap.

Alternatively, if trousers have a side opening, add a strip of tissue to front and back seams.

<u>After</u>

Adjust added tissue as necessary.

Remember to adjust waistband to fit new waist measurements.

Remember to allow plenty of fullness at back of trousers so that doll will be able to sit with ease.

Trousers

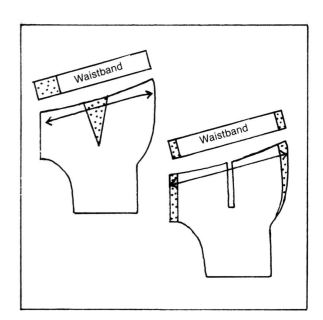

IF PATTERN IS TOO SMALL

PATTERN ALTERATION   - continued

Too narrow around hips?

<u>Before</u>

Pin a strip of tissue to front and back seams or cut up from lower leg at side edge and open out to required width. Pin a strip of tissue to fill gap.

<u>After</u>

Adjust added tissue as necessary.

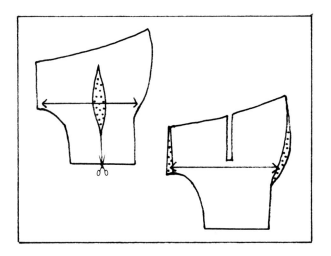

Trousers

IF PATTERN IS TOO SMALL

PATTERN ALTERATION - continued

Too narrow around thigh?

Before

Add a strip of tissue to inside leg seam. This may be a continuation of the increase made over the hips.

Alternatively, cut up from lower edge at sides and open out to required width. Pin a strip of tissue to fill gap.

After

Adjust added tissue as necessary.

Please Note

For bent limb dolls take into consideration the difference between the inside and outer curve leg measurements.

Any addition to the lower leg will need to be reflected in a leg band.

Ensure that the final width of lower leg is sufficient for the trousers to pass over the doll's foot when being dressed.

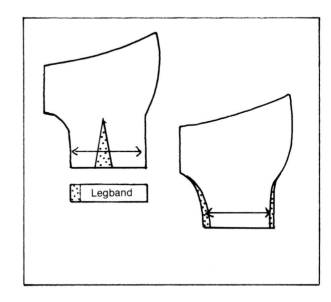

Legband

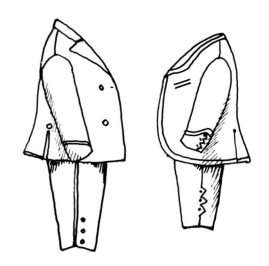

Trousers

PATTERN ALTERATION   - continued

Too short from waist to crutch?

Before

Add a strip of tissue to front and back at waist edge or cut front and back horizontally at hip level and add a strip of tissue.

Remember to keep enough ease in the back depth to allow the doll to sit.

After

Adjust added tissue as necessary.

Too short from crutch to knee?

Before

Add a strip of tissue to lower edge of trouser legs.

Remember to check inside and outside leg measurements of bent limb dolls so that the doll can be dressed with ease.

After

Adjust added tissue as necessary.

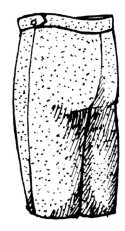

Trousers

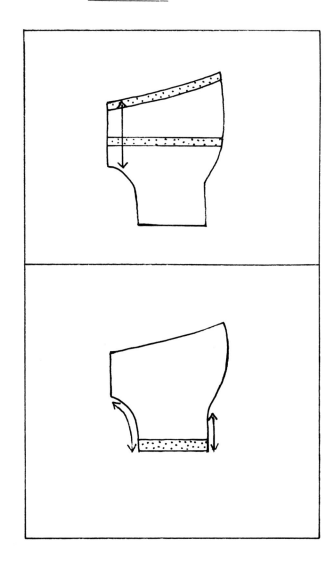

IF PATTERN IS TOO BIG

Construction of Mock-up - Join seams as necessary. Run gathering threads where gathers are indicated. Pin tucks or pleats as necessary. Try on mock-up with right sides against doll's head, wearing wig if applicable, so that any seams or fullness can be adjusted easily.

PATTERN ALTERATION

Too wide from ear to ear over front hairline?

Flat Bonnet

Take tucks in pattern around front edge to reduce fullness evenly around face.

Gathered Bonnet

Either : Decide that extra fullness can be gathered in with greater effect.

or : Trim excess from side edges, tapering toward back, as necessary.

Hat with brim

Crown: Adjust as for Bonnet above, as applicable.

Shaped brim

Trim and shape lower edges of brim and/or fill in top of inner curve with tissue to reduce inner curve measurement. Adjust outer curve to required height of brim.

Hat or Bonnet

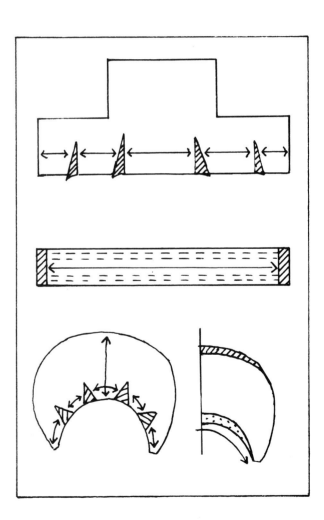

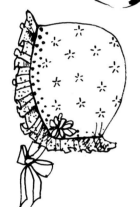

Hat or Bonnet

IF PATTERN IS TOO BIG

PATTERN ALTERATION - continued

Exaggerated hat with close fitting lining

Make any adjustments to lining and reduce hat fullness as applicable.

Pleated or gathered brim

Re-calculate length of pleating or gathering as necessary.

Too wide centre front (hairline) to nape of neck?

Reduce pattern by taking horizontal tucks in main crown and/or back crown or evenly distribute smaller tucks across entire crown.

Too large around head?

Headband

Trim excess from length.

Mobcap or Beret

Trim excess from outer edge of circle.

Too wide from ear to ear across back of neck?

Either : Trim excess from side edges.

or : Make evenly distributed tucks or darts in pattern to reduce fullness.

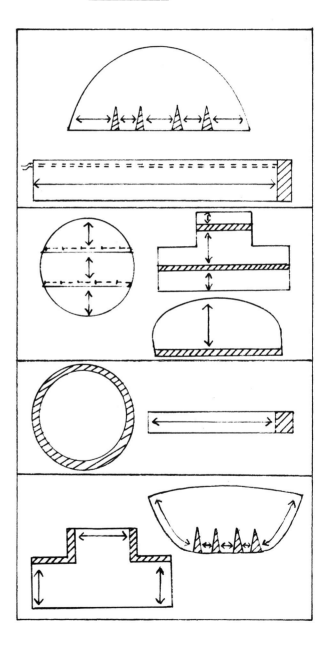

IF PATTERN IS TOO SMALL

Construction of Mock-up - When the pattern pieces appear to be too small it is likely that an assembled mock-up will not fit over the doll. Therefore the majority of alterations will need to be carried out before pinning the pattern pieces together.

The notes under Section 2 are headed "before" and "after" and give instructions for any adjustments to be made before the mock-up is assembled, followed by any further adjustments that may be necessary after the mock-up has been tried on the doll's head.

Join seams as necessary. Run gathering threads where gathers are indicated. Pin tucks or pleats as necessary. Try on mock-up with right sides against doll's head, wearing wig if applicable, so that any seams or fullness can be adjusted easily.

PATTERN ALTERATION

Too narrow from ear to ear over front hairline?

Before

Cut centre line from front edge of crown towards back. Insert tissue into dart, and/or add tissue to side edges.

After

Adjust added tissue as necessary.

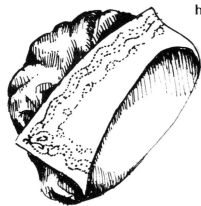

Hat or Bonnet

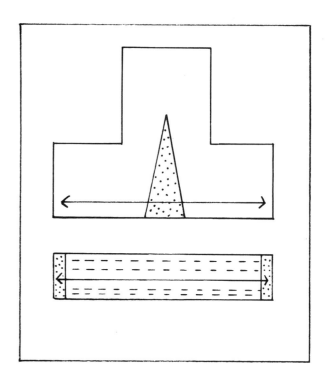

IF PATTERN IS TOO SMALL

PATTERN ALTERATION - continued

Too short centre front (hairline) to nape of neck?

Before

Add tissue to front edge of crown and/or back edges. If there is a separate back crown, adjust depth to correspond with any extra tissue added at back edges.

After

Adjust added tissue as necessary.

Too small around head?

Headband

Before
Add extra tissue to length as required.

After
Adjust added tissue as necessary.

Mob Cap or Beret

Before
Enlarge circumference of circle as required.

After
Adjust circle as necessary.

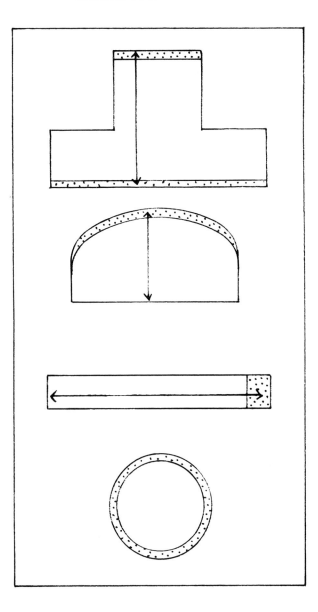

Hat or Bonnet

IF PATTERN IS TOO SMALL

PATTERN ALTERATION - continued

Too narrow from ear to ear across back of neck?

<u>Before</u>

Add extra tissue to side edges or cut centre line from back edge towards front and pin tissue into gap.

<u>After</u>

Adjust added tissue as necessary.

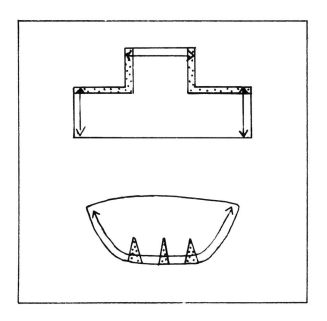

Hat or Bonnet

3
FABRIC, LACE and FASTENINGS

Fabric

FABRIC

Choosing the fabric with which to dress your doll will depend, to a great extent, on whether you are dressing a reproduction doll or your own artist creation, when you will probably be selecting fabric manufactured today, or whether you are dressing an antique doll and are able to find the older fabrics to maintain its authenticity.

Modern Fabrics

Whenever possible, choose modern fabrics with the natural texture of cotton, wool or silk as these create a softer appearance. If the fabric has an overall design make sure the size and style is in proportion to the garment you are making, and the smaller the garment the more important this becomes. There are many cotton prints produced today with smaller designs often in a muted colour. Some of these have the small design printed in a stripe effect and these resemble very closely the old Victorian cotton prints.

For silk, wool, or the mixtures of both, choose the softer shades as strong bright colours often overwhelm the delicate shading of a doll's face. This does not mean that you should ignore the darker hues of navy, brown, maroon or green, all of which would have been found in dolls' clothes of the late nineteenth and early twentieth century. The colour of eyes and hair and the facial expression of the doll will also suggest whether its clothes should be demure white, or soft pastel or a darker colour.

Silk can be bought today in a variety of exclusive textures from fine ribbed silk, to woven coloured checks and small brocade designs in delicate colours. Although the price per metre can be expensive, the authentic look it will give your reproduction doll, apart from the luxury of sewing with a quality fabric, can often outweigh such an expense, especially as you may only need up to half a metre to complete the outfit. Again you may be lucky to find a remnant which could further reduce the cost.

The remnant box of your fabric shop can be a very useful source often producing exactly what you are looking for in the right quantity and of course with the added bonus of a bargain price. Another source of suitable fabric is the furnishing department. Many of the textures of furnishing fabric are quite fine and often made in natural fibres. The designs on finer textures are usually in a smaller proportion and in muted shades reminiscent of the 'old look'. You can also find delicate brocade or water-marked moire taffeta suitable for the more elaborate or fashion dresses.

Cotton sateen, used for curtain lining, comes in a variety of shades and resembles the dresses worn by the cheaper commercial dolls of yesteryear. Use the dull side as the right side and if you feel that the depth of colour is too strong, a short soak in a weak solution of bleach will often lighten the shade. Use a small piece of fabric to experiment with and always thoroughly wet

FABRIC - continued

the fabric before immersing it in the solution to ensure even distribution.

If you feel that new cotton has a lot of dressing in it to keep it crisp and that it is just too stiff, wash the length a couple of times or perhaps use a fabric softener solution. This will make the fabric much softer to handle, especially if you are hand sewing the seams. You can always add a solution of starch or use spray starch after you have made up the dress if you wish to put back some substance to the cotton. Wool and silk will usually be soft enough and will not need this treatment. In fact, silk should only be washed if the manufacturer recommends it and if so, wash with care, do not wring out and always iron when still damp. When ironing silk at any time, use a dry iron with the correct setting. A steam iron, and more seriously, a spluttering steam iron used for pressing during the making up process, can splash the silk and leave a permanent mark.

Velvet is another popular choice of fabric for dolls clothes, especially for boys' trousers. As modern cotton velvet is much coarser than its antique plush counterpart, it is more suitable for medium to larger dolls. Small dolls can be overwhelmed by the texture of velvet and as velvet can fray badly when sewing smaller shapes you often find yourself with a lapful of fluff and bits before you have completed a few seams.

It is better to line velvet dresses or trousers for this not only eliminates laborious oversewing of seam edges but also prevents the fluff from frayed edges sticking to underwear or even socks as you dress your doll.

If after all your searching you cannot find exactly the shade of fabric you want, you can experiment with dyeing. For the small yardage you will be using it is not necessary to make up a large dye bath. Use only a teaspoonful of dye powder, a pint of boiling hot water and two tablespoonsful of salt and add this to a small bowl of very hot water. Use a small piece of old sheeting to find the correct length of time it takes to achieve the right shade. Always soak the fabric well in lukewarm water, do not wring but allow the surplus water to drip away, then immerse the wet fabric in the dye solution to distribute it evenly. Keeping the fabric immersed, stir continuously so that the dye cannot settle in patches. Lace, trimmings and even pearl buttons can be added to the dye solution for toning accessories.

Antique Fabric

As antique fabric can no longer be bought by the yard, your choice is limited to what you can find using already made up clothes or portions of these. Where do you find this elusive fabric? With perseverance! Having dressed antique dolls for collectors for a

Fabric

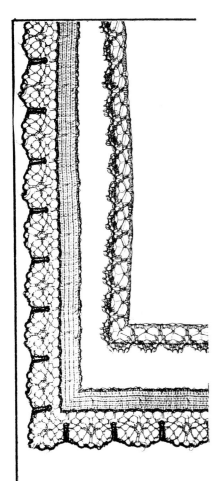

Fabric

FABRIC - continued

number of years and using only authentic fabric, lace and trimmings and even the old brass hooks and eyes, I can only suggest that you become a detective following all the clues that can lead you to find the fabric you are looking for. Such clues can lead you to:

Auction Houses:

Specialist Costume and Textile auctions or the more general local auction can reveal a tea chest or cardboard box full of fascinating items of linen, damaged embroidered tablecloths or traycloths, a baby gown, or oddments of garments - perhaps a lawn undersleeve hand embroidered with whitework or decorated with minutely stitched pin tucks and insertion lace, a bodice without a skirt or vice versa, or with luck, a complete dress with its beautiful trimmings, frills and ribbons.

Charity Shops:

Mention your interest in old fabric and accessories, not forgetting buttons, to the organiser of the shop. Perhaps on a return visit you will be presented with a small bag of 'goodies' that has been put by for you.

Jumble Sales:

As the majority of these sales cater mainly with modern garments and man-made fibres, it is exceptional to find suitable fabric among these clothes.

There is often a separate table carrying oddments as well as household linen and furnishings. It may be there that you will find something of interest, perhaps an artificial silk bedspread, or some guest towels made of cotton.

The bedspread may be heavily machine embroidered in the centre but the surrounding areas are usually large enough for the small pattern pieces of dolls clothes. If the guest towels are made of huckaback cotton, they can be used for plain baby bonnets, or an apron or even a small pinafore. You may also find some buttons or small buckles or a necklace suitable for remaking or selecting beads for earrings. The pearls from a broken necklace can be used as buttons to decorate the front of a dress. Try grouping them in threes with a space between instead of a continuous line.

Specialist Doll Fairs:

Some of the stallholders specialise in old lace and braid, as well as feathers and sprays of flowers. Others may have a basket of old fabric where you could discover just the piece you have been looking for.

Craft Fairs:

You will generally find a stallholder selling old household linen with perhaps some Victorian and Edwardian chemises or underwear or baby gowns. Occasionally you

FABRIC - continued

will find an old garment hanging up which you can examine carefully to see if the fabric is suitable for your doll's clothes. Ask the stallholder if they have more garments available elsewhere as maybe they have left some behind for a variety of reasons. Discuss your interest as this often opens up more avenues than you could have found by yourself.

Maybe the lady making lace pillows has acquired some old fabric along with the lace she is using and has been reluctant to throw it away even though it is not suitable for her pillows. These stallholders often offer lace handkerchiefs as well and these can be used for a variety of decorations on a dress or used to make an entire dress for a miniature doll.

Market Stalls:

Find the trader in second hand clothes and explain your interest. Ask when they will next be in the area and visit the next event in the hope that they have found something of interest in the meantime.

The fabric stall is also worth investigating as some of the bolts of fabric could have come from liquidation stock or factory clearance and include some printed cotton or fine wool, or embroidery anglais lengths.

House Clearance:

Look up your local paper and contact the people advertising house clearance facilities. In general they only deal in furniture removals, but you may get lucky as I was, admittedly a few years ago, when a trunk had been bought without viewing the inside. When it was opened and the inside lid removed, the whole of the lower half was full of antique fabric remnants, tied in bundles. When untied they revealed the familiar cutting out shapes of a sleeve head, or an armhole or neckline which set me wondering what garment had been made from the original length. There were also some half finished garments, started and put away to finish 'some other time' but never returned to. (I think we are all guilty of doing the same even today as impatience sets in when all is not going to plan!) There were some cut-off sleeves - perhaps a keepsake from a favourite dress - and a length of elaborate trimming which had obviously been too good to throw away, ready to adorn another special dress some day. A few collars and cuffs had, unfortunately, been permanently marked along the creases where they had been folded, inspite of the loving care with which they had been stored in tissue paper, now brown with age.

Fabric

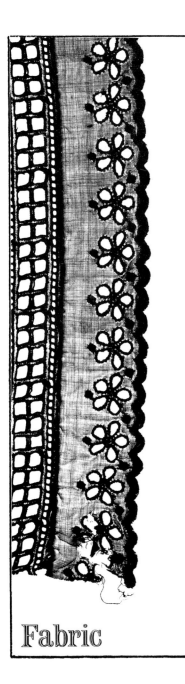

Fabric

FABRIC - continued

I hope these notes have given you enough ideas to explore the countryside for it is always a joy when you have been successful in obtaining a dress, or part of a Victorian or Edwardian garment or a wedding gown skirt with its yards of cream silk. The first thing you notice is the subtle colouring, much softer than the modern dyes. You then discover the construction of the garment with its shaped bodice and boning set into the lining seams, as well as the fine handstitched seams with the raw edges often encased with toning fine silk ribbon. You have to examine the stitches very closely to reassure yourself that they are not machined!! Strangely enough though, you will often find a Victorian dress with hand stitched seams but with an outer frill edged with machine stitching or the shaped seams of a bodice top stitched by machine. Perhaps, with the advent of the sewing machine, the seamstress wished to show that she owned a new machine by adding stitching which would be on view, rather than use it to stitch the inside seams. You would also discover beautifully piped edges where the piping encases the finest cording.

Cutting out the Fabric

Before laying out the pattern pieces on your old fabric, examine it carefully to see where the fabric has faded or perhaps begun to fray or tear due to extra stress. Because you will want to take advantage of any particular decoration or construction detail or incorporate any original needlework in your doll's dress, it is important to discover the straight of the grain so that the pattern pieces will be placed correctly, but remember to take into consideration the proportion of any interesting details so that if included they will not overpower the style of the doll's dress.

When placing the pattern pieces, faded areas can be used so long as they will match or tone in together along a seamline. Try not to join a faded area to a more brightly coloured protected area, especially if such seams would then fall in a prominent part of the dress. It is of course not always possible to avoid differing shades of the original colour but they can be disguised by covering with added lace or trimmings, especially if these can also be extracted from the original garment.

It is likely that you will wish to keep the dusty and discoloured authentic antique look of the fabric and not wash or dry clean the garment. However, if the garment is particularly soiled do not attempt to wash it until you have tested a small piece to discover if the dye will remain fast. Even if it appears to be a fast dye, do not immerse the whole garment in soap suds but unpick the main seams and then wash each piece separately so that any special areas can be given more gentle treatment. That way also you will not have spoilt the whole garment if you discover after all that the dye is not fast and that particular piece has been ruined.

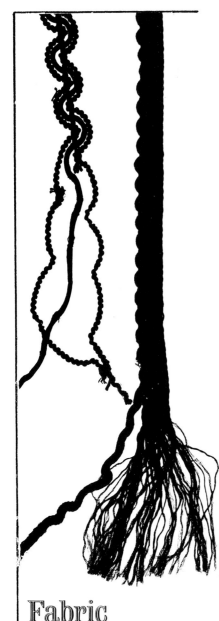

Fabric

FABRIC - continued

Maybe the following ideas will help you identify interesting sections of the old clothes and how you can adapt them to the scale of dolls' clothes.

Jacket or Bodice:

Can the front be used together with the original fastenings?

Is the lower jacket shaped to a point and so become a bodice dress front for a larger doll?

Is the back shaping suitable for a bodice or jacket back?

Has the boning been encased in lining and attached separately to the inner seams? - important if these are not required and must be removed.

Can any piping be used intact - or unpicked for reuse?

Are any decorations (lace, braid or buttons) in the right proportion? Could they be reused? Perhaps the width of the lace can be cut narrower. The cut edge can be incorporated into a seam or covered with insertion lace or fine ribbon. If the braid is too wide, look to see how it is constructed. Many braids are twisted cords - perhaps it can be unravelled to give you several finer strands in just the right proportion for the doll's dress.

Can any fullness at the top of sleeves be used for doll's sleeves? The authenticity of faded and even worn folds in a sleeve has extra effect.

Can the wrist or cuff edges be used to advantage? Often one cuff will be wide enough to cut out the two identical cuffs for your doll's sleeves.

Skirt:

Is the quantity of fabric and the lie of the grain suitable for making the whole garment?

Can the hemline be incorporated as the doll's skirt hemline? You may need to unpick and remove the interlining as this would be too stiff for dolls clothes. The interlining of the old skirts was often a fine buckram and this should be kept for stiffening dolls' hats.

Is there an underfrill of lace? This can be perfect for adding to an elaborate dress for a French doll.

Are there overfrills on the lower half perhaps cut on the cross and bound at edges for decoration? Perfect for the short skirt of a low-waisted doll's dress.

Is there ruching in the upper part which can be incorporated with great effect into a doll's bodice?

Fabric

FABRIC - continued

Baby Gowns:

Is the yoke suitable for narrowing and shortening to fit across a doll's chest and shoulders?

Can the sleeves be shortened from the top, the sleeve head reshaped and reset into the armhole of the recut yoke? Try to leave the lower edge intact as this is usually cuffed and lace edged with fine needlework stitches.

Is the long skirt tucked and lace edged suitable for cutting to a skirt depth?

Can the remaining plain area of the skirt be used for smaller dolls' underwear?

Ladies Nightgowns:

Can the decoration of lace and tucks be used as a basic fabric for a yoke or a chemise or underwear?

Can any frills be unpicked and used as decoration?

Can the main seam of long sleeves be unpicked to allow the whole width of the lower half to be used for two doll's sleeves?

Household Linen:

Old Cotton Sheets: Generally suitable if fine enough. Can be used for linings and for experimenting with dyeing.

Traycloths & Mats: Fine lace and crochet edgings can be unpicked if attached by hand. If the crochet has been attached with a crochet hook for the first row, cut into the fabric around the mat, close to first row. Sometimes woven strands will unravel to release the crochet intact. Cotton or lawn mats can be used for underwear. A hem stitched edge will make an excellent decorative hem.

Handkerchiefs:

Gentlemen's large lawn handkerchiefs can be useful for small dolls' underwear and linings. Ladies smaller and more decorative handkerchiefs can be useful for yokes or collar and cuffs or for underwear, while the larger decorative ones can be used to dress a very small doll.

Ribbons:

Wider ribbons can often provide enough fabric for small dolls' complete garments, using the edge for skirt hems. Also useful for pleated or gathered edgings. If a wide ribbon is too wide yet too short in length, but just the right colour, it can be cut down the middle to give you twice the length. Use a machine overlocking stitch with the smallest setting and a matching thread to neaten the cut edge. With sharp scissors and a steady hand, carefully trim the edge to remove any threads which have not been caught into the overlocking stitches.

FABRIC - continued

Identifying your Fabric and its Characteristics

The natural fabrics of cotton, silk and wool come in various weaves and thicknesses, each being given an identifying name. Some of the more generally known names are:

Cotton

Batiste, calico, cambric, corduroy, dimity, drill, flannelete, gaberdine, gingham, lace, lawn, muslin, organdie, pique, poplin, sateen, satin, seersucker, tulle, velvet, velveteen, voile and winceyette.

Cotton is very easy to sew, does not fray easily and is also easy to cut out since the fabric does not slip away from you when laid out on the table. Cotton will also absorb more dye colour, of course depending on the depth of original colour.

Silk

Brocade, chiffon, douppion, crepe, faille, foulard, georgette, lace, moire, net, organza, satin, shantung, taffeta, tulle, tussore and velvet.

Silk has a lustrous sheer fibre with a natural sheen and excellent draping qualities. The fabric weight can vary from a gossamer chiffon or organza to a heavy brocade.

Silk has always been extensively used for more elaborate doll's clothes, but it can be a problem when it comes to cutting out the small shapes of a doll's proportions. A few tips - use a tablecloth or blanket on the table and lay the silk on this. If the silk has to be folded for cutting out, first press the piece with a warm iron and pin the selvedges together using small fine lace making pins. The warmth from the iron will help the two sides to cling together long enough to cut out your pattern pieces. When laying out, place the pins within the seam allowance so as not to mark the silk where it will show. Make sure your cutting out scissors are very sharp so as not to drag the silk out of place.

Try to sew as much of silk by hand. If using a sewing machine, change the needle for a fresh fine needle and check the tension is not too taut, especially for very fine sheer silk. Always sew with silk thread and only machine a seam when you know it will be correct, as the needle marks will remain after you have unpicked an incorrect seam.

Silk can be handwashed but some of the added processing of silk fabric can mean that it must only be dry cleaned. If you are in doubt, check a small piece before immersing your whole fabric in water. When ironing do not spray with water to dampen as the spots will remain with a permanent outline. Be careful also with your steam iron in case it is inclined to splutter.

Fabric

FABRIC - continued

Silk can be dyed successfully but generally only pastel shades will be achieved without further processing.

Wool

Barathea, boucle, broadcloth, crepe, flannel, wool gaberdine, wool georgette, serge, tweed, velour and whipcord.

Wool is soft to feel and handle, and it is easily moulded and eased into shape by shrink pressing. When ironing, take care not to mark the seam edges on the right side. Wool can also be dyed but any manufacturer's instructions should be followed exactly.

Fabric Characteristics

With the introduction of man-made fibres it is sometimes difficult to tell the difference between fabrics made with natural fibres and those made from polyester or other filament fibres. Since you will prefer to sew with cotton or silk or wool it may be that a remnant you have acquired is difficult to identify. As most fabrics burn in a particular way, it is possible to identify the content of the fibres by cutting off a small corner, and holding it in a pair of tweezers, pass it over the flame of a candle or match.

I have listed several fabrics including some with man made fibres and described the different results achieved when they are burnt.

So that you can visualise these descriptions and recognise the smell being emitted, I suggest you experiment by burning small pieces of fabric which you already know to be made of silk or wool or whatever. Then when testing your unknown fabric in the future you will be able to recognise particular characteristics more easily.

Fabric

FABRIC - continued

IMPORTANT - When making any burning test, take care to protect any surface as well as, of course, yourself.

COTTON

Ignites and burns readily, with smell of burning paper, leaving a small amount of soft grey ash.

LINEN

Slower than cotton to ignite but then burns readily, with smell of burnt paper. Leaves a small amount of grey ash.

WOOL

Burns with difficulty, with smell of burning hair. Leaves crisp black beads of carbon which crush easily. Initially wool will sizzle.

SILK

Burns easily leaving ash. An animal smell is noticeable.

ACETATE

Burns to leave a hard black molten bead, which is easily crushed. Faint smell of acetic acid.

POLYESTER

Melts and burns with a smokey flame to leave a hard bead, which remains very hot. Handle with care.

RAYON

Burns readily with smell of burning paper, and bright flame. Leaves white ash.

Fabric

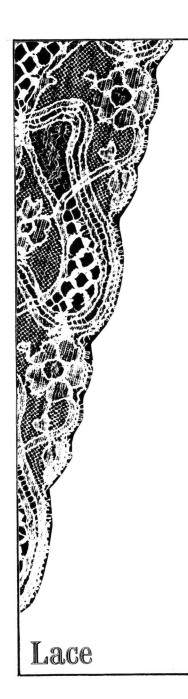

Lace

LACE

Lace plays an important part in the decoration of dolls' clothes with that 'old fashioned look'. It needs to be selected with great care so that the width as well as the design is in proportion to the doll's garment. The smaller the doll the more important this becomes.

There are numerous ways that lace can be used and here are a few suggestions:

As a pleated or gathered edging and attached -

to a neck edge -

- standing up behind a bound edge.
- included into the neck binding seam to fall downwards over the bodice or yoke.
- turning a folded edge at straight edge of lace, gathering through fold and attaching over neck binding on right side.

around shoulder line -

- taper the ends of deep lace and attach into armhole seam.
- stitch to bodice just inside armhole seam and cover raw edge with straight insertion lace or narrow ribbon.
- allow lace to fall over top of sleeve.

to a lower sleeve -

- at wrist edge to fall downwards (especially useful if a finished sleeve turns out to be too short).

to a sleeve to simulate a cuff -

- stitch several layers close together, across the lower edge of a sleeve, facing either upwards or downwards.

to emphasise a cuff -

- stitch to either edge of cuff or to top edge only.

around a yoke -

- stitch around a finished yoke edge and cover the raw edge with straight insertion lace or narrow ribbon. If insertion lace has eyelet holes or an openwork design, ribbon can be threaded through lace for extra effect.

to a bodice to simulate a yoke -

- repeat yoke decoration on a plain bodice for mock yoke effect.

to decorate a bodice -

arrange lace in various directions -
- vertically from either shoulder to centre waist, front and back.
- circle a frill around bodice halfway down and across shoulders.
- from centre shoulder vertically down to waistseam to simulate bretelles or shoulder straps.

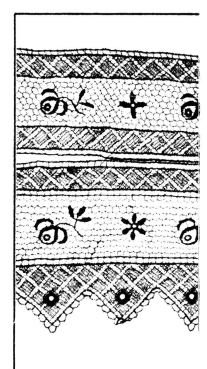

Lace

LACE - continued

a skirt front to simulate an apron -

- stitch to skirt in a half circle from one side of waist seam to the other, equal distance from centre front having lower lace edge just above hemline.

to a skirt frill -

- attach to either edge of a fabric frill.
- fold under top edge, gather through fold and use as a lace frill, having lower edge even with hem.
- slipstitch to the folded edge of horizontal pin tucks.
- to the underside of skirt hem, allowing scalloped edge to fall just below hemline.

The list is endless and I am sure you will discover many other ways of using lace.

If the edging lace you are using is not wide enough, overlap the scalloped edge onto the straight edge of another length of matching lace and join with small running stitches outlining the curve of each scallop. Join as many lengths as needed to reach the required width of lace. The same effect can be reached by joining the straight edges of insertion lace and attaching the straight edge of matching scalloped lace to the final edge.

Another effective use of lace is to cover the dress fabric or coloured lining, especially if the lace has a decorative allover design.

Make sure that the overall design is in proportion to the scale of the doll's dress. Study the lace design and determine where this will show to advantage on the bodice, sleeves and/or skirt.

When you are using a precious piece of antique lace, do not be in a hurry to cut out the pattern pieces. I usually leave them intact on the lace and return to the layout the next day when I can have a fresh look at the design. Only when I am satisfied that the best effect will be achieved, do I cut the lace.

Tack the lace pieces to the right side of the dress fabric or lining and treat as one fabric when joining the seams. However, when overlaying a skirt with lace, it is better to treat the lace as a separate skirt, neatening the lower edge if there is not a natural scallop by attaching an edging of toning narrow scalloped lace, again keeping the design in proportion to the larger piece. Tack the top edge of skirt and lace together and treat as one fabric for any gathering or pleating into the waist seam. Also neaten the waistline opening by slip stitching the lace to the skirt facing or binding.

If you are dressing an antique doll with authentic fabric, always use old lace which will be softer in texture and colour than modern new lace. Minor breaks or tears in the lace can be darned with fine lace maker's thread to avoid any further deterioration.

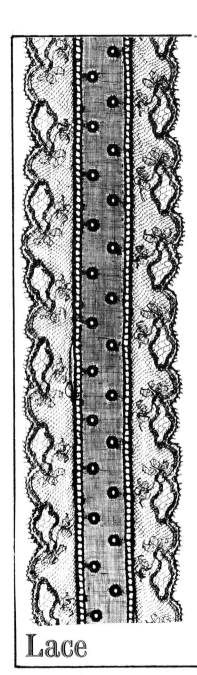

Lace

LACE - continued

Try to identify the old lace you are using. There are many good reference books on lace identification or you may know a friend or a lace dealer who can identify the lace for you. This knowledge will give you much pleasure in dressing your doll. If, after identification of your lace, you feel that it is exceptional, it may be of more historical value as a collector's piece rather than cut it up for decorating your doll's dress.

However, not all of you will be dressing antique dolls in authentic textiles, lovely as they are, and luckily there is still a wide selection of cotton lace available today. If your new lace appears to be too stiff, you can wash it before use to soften the threads. It may be that you need a softer tone than stark white. A weak solution of tea or coffee will produce a light dye from pinky ecru to a deeper cream.

Always thoroughly wet the lace in lukewarm water before immersing it into a dye solution. This ensures that the dye travels quickly into the threads of the lace and produces an evenly distributed colour. Stir the lace in the solution and leave until the required depth of colour is achieved. If you are doubtful of the correct shade, experiment on a strip of old cotton sheeting. A different blend of colour can be achieved by mixing tea and coffee solutions.

You may wish to use a coloured lace to tone or contrast with your dress fabric. A delicate pastel shade of colour can be achieved by mixing a teaspoonful of dye with a pint of hot water and two tablespoonsful of salt. Again you can experiment with a strip of old cotton sheeting to find the correct length of time needed to obtain the shade you are looking for. A cold water dye solution can be equally as successful.

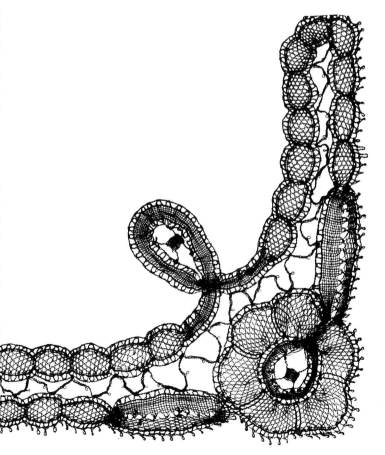

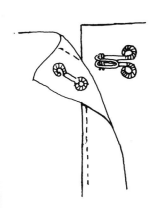

FASTENINGS

Hooks & Eyes

For commercially bought hooks and eyes try to find the smallest possible and it is preferable to buy those with a bar fitting rather than with a circular "eye". The bar fitting is less likely to allow the facing edge of an opening to gape, especially when a dress has a snug fit. Always use a hook fastening at the neck and waist or lower bodice where the skirt is attached so as to have a flatter outline. A press fastener at these points would be more obvious, and not carry so much strain if a close fitting effect is required.

For a decorative effect or to disguise the hook, attach the hook with fine buttonhole stitches in a matching thread to cover the whole metal area.

It may be, however, that you are dressing an antique doll. If you are lucky enough to find hooks or bar fittings still attached to your old fabric and if they are not too large, always re-use these to give extra authenticity to your dress. Perhaps you have found some hooks at the bottom of an old button box but no "eyes" or it is only the hooks that you can salvage from the old fabric, then you will need to make thread loops.

To make a thread loop, use a double thread in a matching colour and work two or three straight stitches over one another in the correct position and just long enough to hold the hook. Work **buttonhole stitches** over these threads, taking care to insert your needle behind the threads and not catch the fabric underneath. When the threads are completely covered, fasten off securely so that the bar will not unravel with use.

Use the same method of sewing but ensure that the length of the initial straight threads are long enough to go around the button. Remember also that as you buttonhole the threads the larger the loop the slightly shorter it becomes. Sometimes on finer fabric it is difficult to control the free standing threads and still maintain the circle of the loop. Use a knitting needle or the flat side of suitable sized scissors to insert into loop to hold the shape and also act as a base to control the evenness of the buttonhole stitches, and keep your sewing needle away from the main fabric.

You may also need to use thread loops for fastening buttons when a buttonhole will not be suitable either for the fabric or for the style of garment.

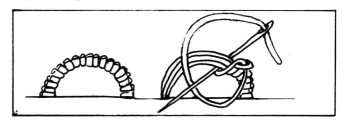

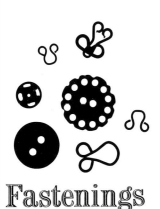

Fastenings

FASTENINGS - continued

If you find your dress to be a snug fit and there is very little overlap at an opening, you could try placing your hooks, two at a time, alternately down each side edge. Work alternate thread loops to correspond. This will hold the opening edges together with less strain. On the right side you can add an overlapping braid or a pleated edging to hide the opening and add decoration as well.

Press Fasteners

Press fasteners should be selected when the correct size of hooks are not available. Sew the fasteners with matching thread and use the thinner pointed stud for attaching to the top overlapping facing and the thicker receiving stud to the underlap facing. If you wish to disguise the fasteners, cut a small circle of dress fabric, or toning silk if the fabric will be too cumbersome, and run a gathering line around the outer edge. Place the stud in the centre and draw up the circle to the underneath.

Sew the upper and lower studs in the usual manner and you will find that the pointed stud will slot into the receiving stud through the covering fabric without difficulty.

The right side of the dress opening can be decorated by adding buttons over the press fasteners, especially if they are showing through any finer fabric.

Rouleau loops for small buttons

A rouleau strip is formed by a length of bias fabric sewn to form a long narrow tube.

Cut the width of the bias strip to measure four times the width of the required finished loops. Make sure the length is sufficient to make all the loops at the same time. Be extra generous rather than skimp the length. Fold the strip in half lengthways with right sides together and stitch seam through the centre length. Trim one end to a point. Thread a bodkin or long blunt needle with double thread and sew securely to pointed end. This will prevent the thread escaping from the bodkin or needle while the rouleau is being drawn through to the right side. Place the needle, eye first into tube and gently ease the rouleau over the thread until the needle and thread have passed through to the other end, turning the rouleau to the right side as it travels. Cut off drawing thread and press the length of tubing.

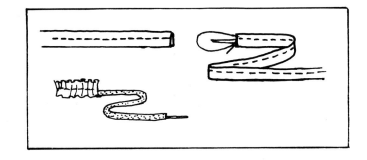

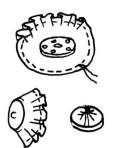

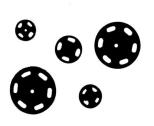

Fastenings

FASTENINGS - continued

To fix the rouleau loops in place - working on the right side place each loop in the correct position allowing enough loop to encircle the button and having the ends tacked to the seam allowance and the loops facing inwards. Use a facing strip to encase the ends within the seam allowance. Stitch seam and turn facing to wrong side and hem in place. The loops will now extend beyond the finished edge ready to hold the buttons.

The same procedure will apply if the bodice is being fully lined when the extra facing strip will be unnecessary.

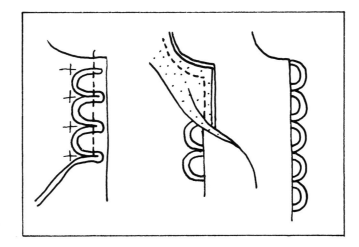

Buttons

Luckily there are still suppliers of small pearl buttons which are used extensively for dolls clothes, but it is still fun to discover the button box in a second hand or charity shop or even a garage sale. Whenever I find one I always ask for a large dish or plate so that I can transfer all the buttons gradually turning a handful at a time because it is often the wrong side of the button which will reveal the iridescent shine of pearl and it is always at the bottom of the box that you find all the small buttons, as well as the odd hook and sometimes but not very often, the eyes but never a matching pair! You will sometimes find the very small press fasteners that alas are no longer made today. Other finds can often be a decorative half of a small clasp or beads or a small buckle, all of which can be added to your own 'trimming' box knowing that one day it will be 'just right' for that particular dress, or outfit.

Always use the size of button which is in proportion to the style of the garment. If you are dyeing a fabric to obtain a particular shade of colour, you can add pearl buttons to the dye water to obtain a toning colour.

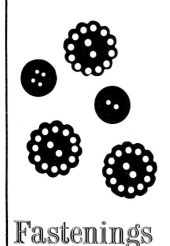

Fastenings

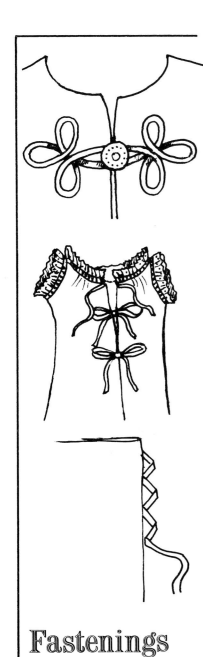

FASTENINGS - continued

If you are unable to find just the right coloured button, you can cover a set of small ordinary buttons in matching fabric or contrast silk. Cut a circle of fabric slightly larger than the button and run a gathering line around the outer circle. Place the button to the wrong side and draw up the gathering thread to enclose the button. Fasten off securely.

If you prefer a more professional finish, you can arrange for the covered buttons to be made commercially.

Buttonholes

As the facings on doll's clothes are usually quite narrow, it is easier to work vertical buttonholes rather than the more conventional horizontal buttonholes that we would use for our own clothes.

Place the button in the position required and mark the width of the button with two pins placed horizontally to the opening edge. Using small pointed sharp scissors, make an incision in the centre of the two pins and snip first towards one pin and then turn and snip towards the second pin. This method will prevent the scissors from cutting more fabric than necessary and working in either direction will stop the scissors exactly at the pins and no further. Make sure that the point of the scissors penetrates both thicknesses of the facing edge and test the button through the cut to check that the buttonhole will be large enough.

Use a single matching thread, run small stitches along cut edge and oversew raw edges to the stitching line. Using matching thread double, work buttonhole stitches closely around cut to cover oversewn edge. Fasten thread securely, to prevent stitches unravelling with use.

If you are in doubt as to whether the fabric you are using will fray excessively and not make a neat buttonhole, try a sample buttonhole on a scrap of fabric. Remember to use and cut the buttonhole with double fabric to represent a faced edge. You will soon learn all the problems your fabric could give you without having spoilt your newly completed dressmaking.

Alternative suggestions for fastenings

- Use narrow cord to make frogging and fasten with a fancy button.

- Use narrow ribbons and stitch to inside of facing at intervals down opening edge and tie into bows. Very convenient for a petticoat bodice that does not quite meet at the back opening, when cotton tape can be substituted for ribbon.

- For very small garments when rouleau loops could prove too cumbersome, make the loops with very narrow silk or corded ribbon.

Fastenings

4

GENERAL SEWING TECHNIQUES

GENERAL SEWING TECHNIQUES

PLEATS

A pleat is a parallel fold of fabric pressed to one side. The amount of fabric used represents three times the width of each finished pleat.

To ensure the correct amount of fabric to be pleated, multiply the required finished width by three and add in any allowance necessary for the joining of seams. The width of the finished pleat can then be decided, bearing in mind that the narrower the pleat the more pleats will be formed with a closer effect. Similarly the wider the pleats the less there will be.

Depending in which direction the fold of the pleat is facing, pleats are identified thus:

Knife Pleats - Pleats with the folds facing in the same direction, either left or right.

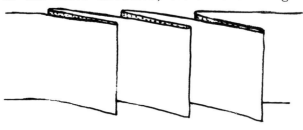

Box Pleats - Knife pleats which fold in opposite directions away from each other, on the right side.

Inverted Pleats - Knife pleats with the folds turned towards each other to meet edge to edge on the right side.

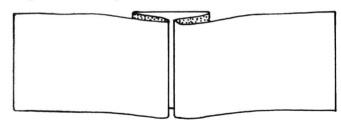

Unpressed Pleats - Any of the above formation of pleats, but with the vertical folds unpressed.

Pleats

How to Prepare Knife Pleats

Decide on the width of finished pleat and, with pins, mark out this width across top of fabric (lines **a, b, c, d,** etc). Fold on line **b** down straight grain of fabric. Place fold line **b** onto line **d** on the right side, causing line **c** to fold along line **a** on the wrong side. Continue with next pleat by folding line **e** to line **g** causing line **f** to fold along line **d** on the wrong side. Continue pleating to end of fabric, making sure that any joins lie along the inside fold so that the seams will not be visible.

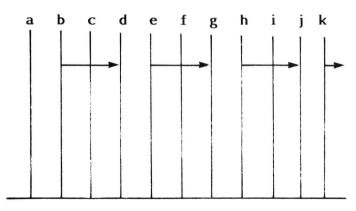

Reverse sequence for knife pleats facing left

Pleat in direction of arrows

How to Prepare Box Pleats

Decide on the width of finished pleat and with pins mark out this width across top of fabric (lines **a, b, c, d,** etc).

With right side facing, fold line **c** and place fold on line **a**. Fold line **e** and place fold on line **g**, thus causing fold lines **b** and **f** to meet on the wrong side on line **d**. Continue by folding line **i** and place on line **g** and folding line **k** and place on line **m**, causing fold lines **h** and **l** to meet on the wrong side on line **j**.

Continue to make box pleats to end of fabric.

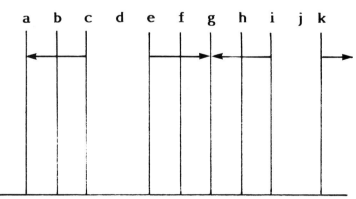

Pleat in direction of arrows

Pleats

PLEATS - continued

How to Prepare Inverted Pleats

Inverted pleats are usually made singly to take up areas of fullness evenly when full pleating is not required, otherwise inverted pleats made one after the other will look like box pleats.

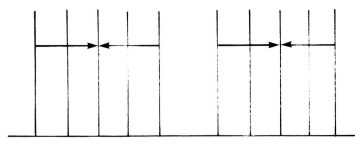

Pleat in direction of arrows

How to prepare a combination of Knife and Box Pleats

The combination of knife and box pleats is often included into the back of a skirt to create extra fullness.

Fold line **c** and place on line **a,** fold line **e** and place fold half way between line **c** and **d.** Fold line **g** and place fold half way between lines **h** and **i.** Fold line **i** and place on line **k.** Repeat the sequence placing fold line **m** onto line **k** and so on. This method produces one knife pleat either side of a full box pleat. Further knife pleats overlapped at the top edge can be formed in between each box pleat to create a fuller flare towards the hem.

When joining overlapped pleats to the flat edge of a bodice, any additional fullness can be eased into seam with a short gathering line along top of pleats.

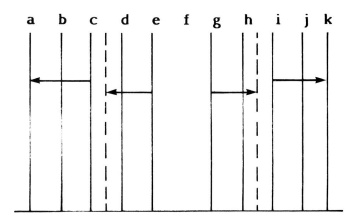

Pleat in direction of arrows

Pleats

Pleats

PLEATS - continued

Preparing a Skirt for Pleating

Generally try to cut a continuous length of fabric to be joined with one seam, placed either at centre back or where an opening is required. However, when several seams are necessary, either through lack of fabric width or when panels are required, join the seam containing the opening first and any other seams but the last. Neaten the skirt opening. Turn up a hem, leaving a short section unfinished at open ends. Press hem edge. Form pleats while fabric is flat, keeping seams towards a back fold. Press pleats. Open out hem and stitch final seam. Complete hem and press final pleat.

Alternatively all the seams can be joined to form a circle of fabric and the hem turned up before pleating. This method could be a little restricting when pleating a skirt for a small doll.

Lining a Pleated Skirt

If a lining is to be added to the skirt, this can be attached before pleating and so avoid a separate hem.

Cut equal retangles for skirt and lining. Decide on the depth of hem and cut off the equivalent hem depth from the lower edge of lining only. With right sides together, join skirt to lining along lower edge. Press seam towards lining. Placing lining behind skirt, tack the top raw edges together. A natural hem will then form at the lower edge. Press hem edge firmly.

While the skirt is flat, make whatever pleats are required, leaving a short amount flat at either edge of skirt so that the final seam can be joined. Remove tacking from top edge, open out skirt and lining and stitch back seam in one operation. If an opening is required, start and end seam the appropriate amount in from each top edge.

Refold skirt and lining together and complete final pleats over back seam. Slipstich lining to skirt at opening edge. Stitch pleats in place along top edge of skirt, ready to attach to bodice or waistband.

Preparing a Pleated Edging or Frill

Prepare a continuous length of fabric for the frill, cut to the finished depth required plus the top seam and hem allowances.

The lower edge should be narrowly hemmed by hand or with a fine machine stitch. If the frill is not to be joined into a circle, then also hem the short ends.

If the fabric is particularly fine, hemming a long continuous length can be tedious and time consuming. Cut the required depth double plus the top seam allowances. Fold in half lengthways with raw edges even at the top and press the folded edge.

Having prepared the length in either manner, the pleats can be marked out and pressed as required.

PLEATS - continued

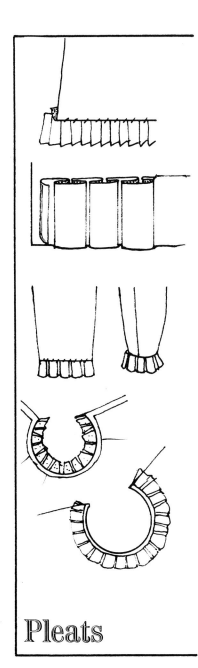

Pleats

There are various methods you can use to attach a pleated edging or frill.

Skirt Flounce: (attached to lower edge to lengthen). Fold under seam allowance of lower edge of skirt. Place folded edge over seam line of pleating and slipstitch in place. On wrong side oversew raw edges.

Skirt Frill: Place wrong side of pleating to right side of skirt, having lower edge even with skirt hem, and tack in place along top seam line of pleating. Cover raw edge of pleating with braid, narrow ribbon or straight edged lace.

Sleeve Edging: If possible join the pleating to the sleeve whilst flat and before the underarm seam is joined.

If however the pleating is being added to a two part coat style sleeve then join the pleating into a circle and slipstitch to inside of finished sleeve edge.

Neck Edging: If pleating is to either stand up or fall around the neck secured with an inside facing, then fit the pleating around the neck edge of bodice or yoke, place the crossway facing strip over the pleating and stitch the seam. Turn the facing to the wrong side and hem in place. Press the pleating in the required direction.

Decorating a Pleated Skirt

Deep lace can be attached to a skirt while the rectangle is flat and the pleats formed to include the overlaid lace.

A narrower lace can be stitched to the lower half of the flat skirt, with the scalloped edge even or just above the skirt hem. The straight top edge of the lace can be covered with narrow ribbon or braid, or if the lace has a regular openwork design, a sequence of spaces can be used to thread a toning or contrast narrow ribbon.

Deep lace can also be gathered and tacked to the top raw edge of ready formed pleats to fall free, with the scalloped edge even or just above the finished skirt hem.

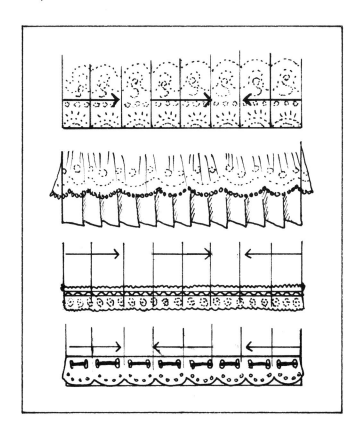

GATHERS AND TUCKS

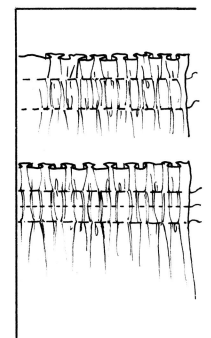

Gathering has the effect of adding fullness with softness and is used in many areas of dolls clothes. The gathers can be stitched by hand using a thread slightly longer than the width to be gathered or by machine using the longest stitch and leaving long threads at the beginning and end of the stitching lines.

If you are in doubt as to how full the gathers will look when given a rectangle to cut for a skirt or the width of a full sleeve, you can experiment and decide the fullness beforehand. Cut a 6" (15cm) length of fabric and run two gathering lines. Draw up the fullness and decide how full you would like the section to be. Measure the width of the reduced gathered section. You can now calculate how wide your fabric will need to be to achieve that fullness.

For example, if your 6" (15cm) width has reduced to 2" (5cm), measure the lower edge of the bodice or around the armhole and then for every 2" (5cm) of this measurement you will need 6" (15cm) of fabric to gather up. (That is - for a 10" (25cm) waistline you will need 30" (75cm) width of fabric.)

Divide the width to be gathered into half and quarters and mark the sections with vertically facing pins. Stitch two rows of gathers, one just above and one just below the seamline. If the width to be gathered is particularly wide then gather up each quarter section separately. You will then have more control over the distribution of fullness and

also there will be less strain on the gathering threads as they are pulled taut.

When gathers are hand stitched pull the two threads together. When the gathers are machine stitched use the longest stitch on your machine, and draw up the bobbin threads only and always ensure that similar threads are drawn up along the entire width of the fabric. If you inadvertently pull from the other end and pick up the other thread of machine made gathers, you can lock the stitches and you will be unable to draw up the fullness.

You can discover how frustrating this can be by stitching two rows of gathers along a small sample of fabric. Pull the top thread from one end and the underneath thread from the other end. You will now see how the stitches lock to prevent any further fullness being gathered.

Always draw up the total fullness as tightly as possible and press the gathers to set the folds. This will help to keep the folds within the two stitching lines and they will be easier to distribute along the width of the straight edge to which they are being joined. Have the gathered edge towards you and with right sides together, pin and distribute the gathers to match the straight edge to which they are being joined. Place the pins vertically upwards with the sharp end over the raw edges. Secure the pulled threads in a figure of eight over pins at either end.

Gathers and Tucks

GATHERS AND TUCKS - continued

Stitch the seam through the centre of the two rows of gathers using a medium stitch width and working slowly over the pins which can be removed after sewing. Pull out the lower gathered thread which will be showing on the right side below the seam. By using this method you will see that the gathers are evenly distributed and there will be no puckering of the fullness which so often happens when only one gathering line is stitched instead of two.

Gathering along weft or warp of fabric

There is also a difference in the effect of gathers that are stitched along the weft and warp of the fabric. It is usual to cut the fabric with the width following the weft threads which are at right angles to the selvedge (warp threads). Gathering lines following the weft will lie flat and press into neat folds. Gathering lines following the warp will not lie as flat and the folds will be more rounded. To demonstrate the different effect, cut a square of fabric and run gathering lines along the weft and warp threads. Pull up fullness and see the difference in the lie of the gathers. If you have no selvedge edge to guide you it is useful to try out this method if you want to discover the lie of the fabric. Also the warp threads are usually slightly thicker than the weft threads as the former take the strain when the fabric is being woven.

GAUGING

A decorative way of drawing in fullness into a narrow space.

Work several parallel lines of evenly spaced stitches, long on top and short on the wrong side, measuring about $\frac{1}{4}$" apart, making sure that the stitches in each row come exactly under one another so that when the fullness is pulled tight the folds are parallel to each other. Draw up the fullness to the required width and secure each end to hold gauging in a permanent shape. The width of each stitching line can either be even to form a box of gathers or each stitching line can diminish evenly down to a point.

A ruched plastron front can also be prepared in this way, drawing up the fullness to fit a lining shape. Often ruched fronts are also interspaced with tucks when a gathering line will hold the tuck in place and the folded edge protrude in a fluted effect when the gathers are drawn up.

Another alternative plastron can be made by making small box pleats vertically down the rectangle and then opening out the pleats, run 3 or 4 gauging lines at the top, centre and lower edge of the plastron. The top edge can be folded over and the first line of stitching will encase the raw edge to give a neat finish when the gathers are drawn up. Lace can also be incorporated at the back of the top fold for greater decoration.

Gathers and Tucks

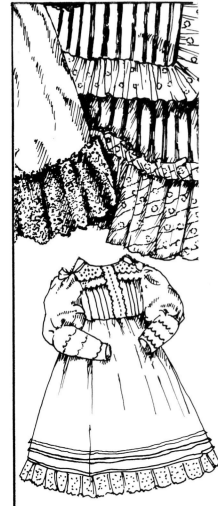

GATHERS AND TUCKS - continued

FRILLS

The notes on Preparing an Edging in the Pleating section also applies to the preparation of frills. The only exception is when frills are applied as a flounce. The gathering lines are placed a little below the top edge which can be hemmed or finished off to match the lower edge. The flounce then has frills forming either side of the stitching line. Any gathering threads should be removed after stitching.

The length of fabric to be gathered can be cut on the straight or crossways on a bias. Straight frills fall closer to a flat fabric to which they are joined and are generally applied to add length to a skirt or sleeve.

Bias cut frills, while using more fabric, have extra flare and stand away from a flat fabric. They are very decorative when overlaid on a skirt or sleeve or edged around a yoke or bonnet. If a striped fabric is used, the diagonal effect will have a decorative contrast to the main fabric.

TUCKS

Tucks can be used almost anywhere on a doll's dress or underwear, or can be used to shorten a bodice, sleeve or skirt, being an easier method than unpicking and correcting an already completed garment while at the same time being decorative.

Pin tucks are the narrowest form being less than 1/8" (3mm) wide and have a small distance between them. As they often cover the whole area of a bodice or yoke, it is easier to prepare the tucks on a rectangle of fabric and then place the pattern pieces in the correct position over the tucked area for cutting out.

Larger tucks can be evenly spaced vertically or horizontally, or have the edges overlapping slightly for a closer effect. Another way of treating tucks is to press them centrally to resemble pleats - this method is often used for a bloused front plastron which is not attached to a lining.

To ensure that tucks are on the straight of the grain and lying either horizontally or vertically in even widths, use a guide cut from stiff card to measure out the distance between the tucks as well as the width of the tucks themselves.

Tucks can also be prepared in a more decorative form as shell tucks. (See Decorative Stitches)

Gathers and Tucks

USING PINS

When using pins to secure fabric edges ready for sewing or preparing pleats or gathers, the direction in which the pins are placed can help with quicker sewing and prevent having to stop every few stitches to remove another pin, especially when you are concentrating on achieving an even distribution of gathers, or the flat lay of pleats or perhaps preventing the top edges or a fold from being caught into the stitching line.

Use only the best quality steel dressmaker pins or fine lacemakers pins so that your fabric is not marked by a coarser quality of pin. The glassheaded long pins can be used on openwork fabrics or for attaching lace when normal pins can be "lost" from view, or fall out more easily.

For Gathers:

When joining gathered fabric to a flat fabric, work with the gathers towards you and place the pins at right angles to the horizontal raw edges and parallel to the folds of the gathers, with the sharp end pointing towards the raw edges. Secure the gathers at intervals stroking the folds straight between each pin. The two end pins on which you wind the excess drawing thread should also point in the same direction.

You can then stitch through the two gathering lines by hand or by machine, and remove the pins after sewing.

For Pleats:

When forming pleats hold the top edges of each fold with a pin at right angles to the horizontal raw edge and parallel with the fold line, with the sharp end pointing towards the raw edge.

To secure the pleat fold evenly to the lower edge, place the pins horizontally at right angles to the fold so that all three thicknesses of fabric are held in place and ensure the correct hang of the skirt when finished. The pleat folds can then be tacked while the pins are in place and removed after tacking.

Do not press pleats while the pins are in place as the pressure can permanently mark the fabric with the indentation of the pins.

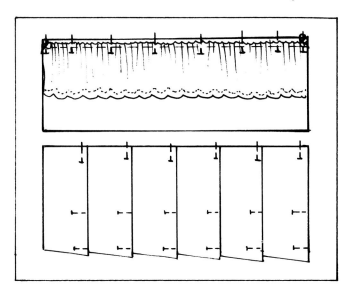

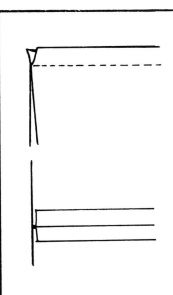

SEAMS

The general seam for doll's clothes is a flat plain seam, joining two raw edges together and pressing the seam open. When one of the edges is more curved, care should be taken to ease any fullness against a flat edge using pins at right angles to the edge so that the natural bias of the seam can be handled at smaller intervals. The seam allowance of curved seams should always be snipped to allow the fabric to lie flat.

Other types of seam are a French seam and a Run-and-Fell seam. These are very suitable for doll's clothes as they prevent the edges from unravelling, being encased in the stitched seam and also they can be made to the narrowest width.

French Seam:

With wrong sides together, stitch a seam $\frac{1}{4}$" (6mm) in from the raw edge. Trim close to stitching and press seam towards one side. Fold on the stitching line right sides together and stitch a second seam encasing the raw edges of the previous seam. Press finished seam towards one side.

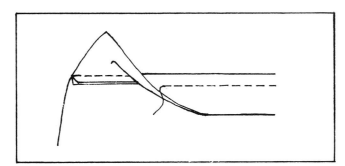

Run and Fell Seam:

With right sides together, stitch a plain seam of $\frac{1}{4}$" (6mm) width. Press to one side. Trim the under seam allowance to half the width, fold under the top seam allowance and hem flat, encasing the trimmed edge. Press seam flat.

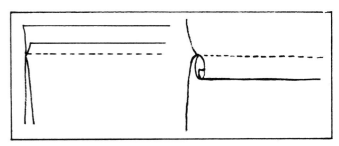

Slip Stitch:

This is a stitch used for attaching self trim or braid or ribbon so that the stitches will not show on the right side.

Work along the edge or fold taking a small stitch from the top and underside working a few running stitches at a time. Do not pull the stitching thread too tightly otherwise the fabric to which the trim is attached will pucker.

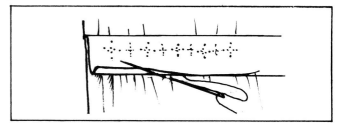

Seams

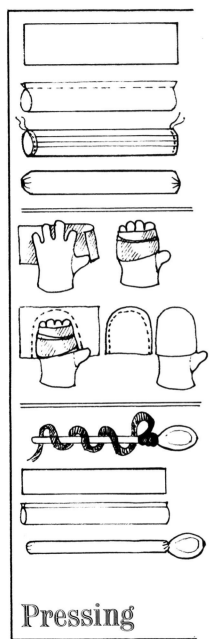

Pressing

PRESSING

As with all dressmaking, it is important to press all seams as you work along. Even more so if the clothes are for an antique doll and need to represent the original clothes which would have by now been quite flattened or sculptured into the doll's shape.

With the scale of clothes for smaller dolls there will be times when the ironing board is inadequate so a sleeve board can prove to be a good substitute. Also a roll pad and hand pad can be useful for moulding the smaller seams of shaped bodices, darts, and the gathers or pleats at a sleeve head.

They are also invaluable for supporting soft velvet when the seams should be lightly pressed or even steamed flat. Such ironing pads can be easily made up from pieces of hard wearing cotton and filled with soft old blanket pieces or cut up soft cloth. If a firmer base is preferred then the pad can be filled with tightly packed sand or bran, when strong ticking fabric should be used for the lining.

To make a Roll Pad - Cut a rectangle 10" x 8" (25cm x 20 cm) of cotton. With right sides together, join the long length. Trim the seam and press open. Turn the outer edges under and run a line of gathers over turnings. At one end pull up gathers and secure thread. Fill pad with selected filling, well packed for a firm base. Draw up gathers at other end and secure thread.

Oversew gathered edges for extra strength when the filling is sand or bran.

To make a Hand Pad - This can be made around an old glove that extends over the wrist.

Place the glove on your hand and keeping fingers together, wrap a strip of soft old blanket, wide enough to fit from base of thumb to tips of fingers, around your gloved hand. Fasten blanket edges at top and bottom.

Lay your gloved hand onto a piece of paper and trace the outline of the blanket pad. Cut out two cotton sections from the traced shape. Join outer seam, turn to right side and place over padded glove. Turn under lower edge and hem outer cover to glove encasing blanket edge.

(An oven glove can be a good substitute for use in general areas, but lacks the flexibility for reaching into those awkward small corners that a covered close fitting glove would give you.)

To make a Stick Pad - Even with these shaped pads, there is always the problem of pressing a narrow finished sleeve and avoiding the crease formed when a sleeve is pressed flat. Use a handle from a wooden spoon, or a piece of broom handle or dowelling for a rounded base. Cut a strip of blanket or thick soft fabric and bind handle or dowelling. Make a cotton covering the length of the stick. Draw up and fasten ends securely.

CUTTING ON THE BIAS

Cutting on the bias or the cross is the method of cutting fabric on a slant so that it is more flexible and stretches to the shape of a curve, especially when used for binding or facing an edge.

To find the true bias of the fabric, make a diagonal fold so that the selvedge or vertical straight of fabric is at right angles to the horizontal straight of fabric. The fold line formed is the line of true bias and all strips of crossways fabric should be cut parallel to this line, measuring out the correct width of each strip. When it is necessary to join bias strips, pin the strips at right angles to each other so that the stitching line is following the straight of the fabric. Trim off the excess points after the seam has been pressed open.

Always handle fabric cut on a bias with care so as not to stretch the edge, as once stretched, the fabric will not return to its original state.

A half bias, which is half the angle of a true bias, is often found along the edge of a panel in a gored or flared skirt for a fashion doll or a Gibson Girl. It can be used with great effect when the gores of a panelled skirt are cut with one edge on the straight and the other on the half-bias. Such panels are joined in sequence attaching a bias edge to a straight edge causing the bias fabric to roll in a fold over the seam. The centre back edges are usually both on a bias to form an extra flare, and roll towards the back seam like an inverted pleat.

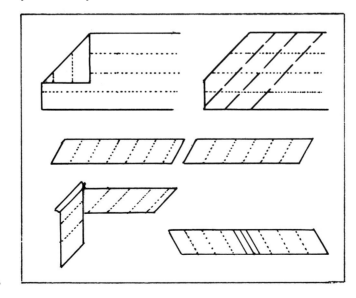

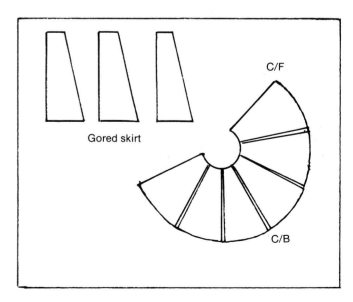

Gored skirt

C/F

C/B

Cutting
on the
Bias

BINDING A NECK

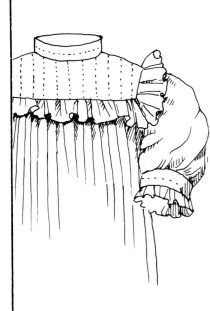

When binding a doll's neck edge or making a mandarin collar, cut the width of the bias strip equal to twice the width of the finished binding plus the seam allowance at either edge.

Fold the strip in half lengthways and tack the raw edges together.

Place the raw edges of bias strip even with the raw edge of neckline on the right side. Slightly stretching the bias tack in place within the seam allowance. Stitch seam. Snip seam allowance around centre curve. Turn bias to wrong side and hem folded edge to stitching line.

This method will always produce a regular width of binding which is sometimes more difficult to achieve with the conventional open binding where the seam allowance has to be turned in and hemmed to the more abrupt curve of a doll's neckline, often resulting in a puckered edge right in the front of the dress.

The same method can be used when facing a neckline that has an attached collar. Tack the collar in place. Tack the folded bias over the collar. Stitch seam through all thicknesses. Snip seam allowance around centre curve. Turn the bias to wrong side and hem fold to wrong side, taking small stitches that do not show through to the right side. Do not sew these stitches too tightly so as to allow the stretch of the bias to follow the neckline curve and lie flat.

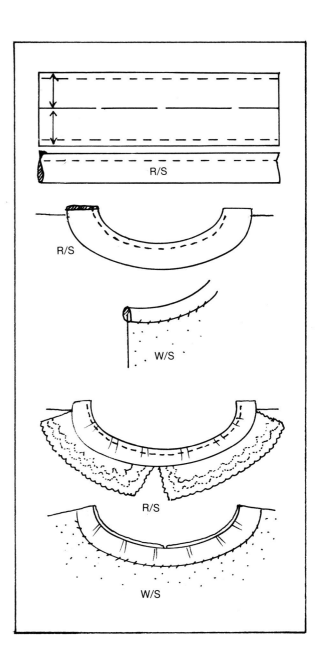

Binding
a Neck

FINISHING SKIRT OPENINGS

There are several ways to neaten the edges of a skirt opening, depending on the complexity of the bodice to which the skirt is being joined, as well as the thickness of the fabric and whether a lace overskirt or a lining is being added.

Plain or gathered skirt with back seam

Stitch back seam leaving appropriate amount of opening at top. Press back seam open.

Turn under 2mm of each seam allowance and secure turning with small running stitches. Slipstitch turned edges in place along opening edges.

To join skirt to a simple bodice, have the opening edges even with the faced edges of back bodice. Stitch waist seam. You will notice that as the bodice is overlapped to fasten, a small pleat is formed at the centre back of skirt.

Opening edge of a pleated skirt

Opening edges should fall along the back fold of a pleat.

Single Fabric

a)   Oversew or stitch back to neaten edges.

or b)   If the opening is not the extension of a stitched seam, cut back fold of pleat to required depth and oversew raw edges.

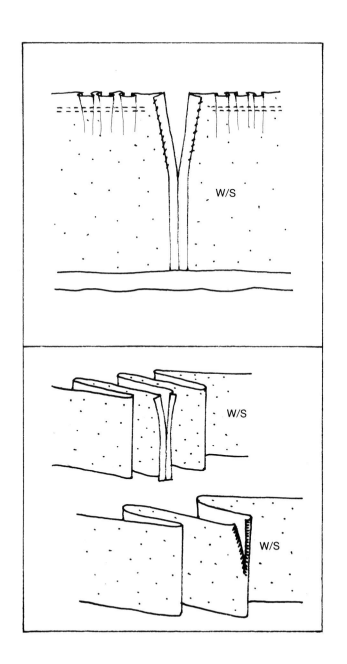

FINISHING SKIRT OPENINGS - continued

Double Fabric

(overlaid with lace and/or backed with a lining)

a)   Oversew raw edges of opening together.
or
b)   Fold under lace (or lining) and slipstitch to skirt.
or
c)   Add a strip of straight binding to either edge of opening (suitable for fine fabrics).

To join pleated skirt to a bodice, the edge of the overlap of bodice should be even with the front fold of the pleat and the underlap of bodice even with the back fold opening. The pleat will then form naturally as the bodice is overlapped to fasten.

On some of the more elaborate French style dresses, a pleated skirt is added to a jacket style bodice with a ruched plastron front. Neaten the opening edges using any of the above methods as appropriate. When joining the skirt to the jacket and plastron front, ensure that the fastenings of the overlapping jacket edge onto the plastron front are in line with the skirt opening and that the pleat lies in the correct direction according to the overlap of the jacket.

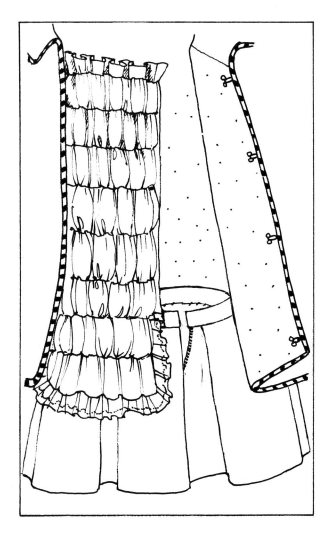

Finishing
Skirt
Openings

Bound Opening

A neat finish when an opening is slit down from top edge and is not an extension of a stitched seam.

If you are not familiar with this type of opening, you should use a piece of practice fabric and experiment before cutting your garment to discover the way the fabric behaves when a slit is opened out horizontally and how to pivot the seam so as not to pucker the garment.

Cut a strip of matching bias fabric, 4cm wide and slightly longer than twice the depth of the slit. Fold under seam allowance of binding on both edges of length and press. Reinforce slit for 2cm either side of point with small running stitches about 1mm away from raw edge.

With the garment towards you and the slit opened out horizontally, open out one folded edge of bias strip and with right sides together, tack strip to garment.

Ensure that the seam allowances of the garment and strip are even at each opening end but as you reach the point, the garment seam allowance tapers to almost nothing yet follows the crease line of the bias strip. It may help to press the slit edges from point to top and match this crease line with the crease line of bias strip. Stitch seam, pivoting at lower point and taking care not to stitch in any of the fullness of the garment as you turn.

On the wrong side of garment, hem the folded edge of bias strip along the stitching line, taking up the stitches only as you hem so that on the right side the seam will be invisible.

Press the binding of the overlapping edge of garment to the wrong side and leave the underlapping edge extended. You will now notice that on the right side of garment the opening lies flat and there should be no puckering at the lower point.

When joining the skirt to a bodice, match the bodice faced edges to the skirt opening so that a continuous overlap will occur as the bodice is fastened.

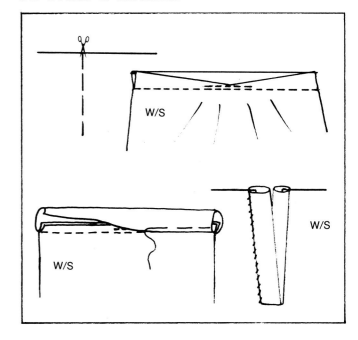

Finishing Skirt Openings

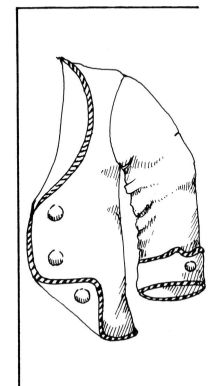

PIPING AN EDGE

Normally when an edge is to be piped, the piping is encased between the general seam and stitched through all thicknesses to allow the piping to extend beyond the seam on the right side. This is the method to follow if it is an inner seam such as the vertical seams of a bodice or skirt or around an armhole.

However, on studying antique dolls clothes, particularly those on French dolls, it is often the outer edges of a jacket front, collar or sleeve and cuff edges that have been piped in a contrast fabric, and the piping has been added after the garment has been constructed. This is not only an easy way of piping an edge although it requires some neat hand sewing, but also is a method of adding extra decoration after you have finished the garment, without having to undo any seams.

To prepare the piping for either method of construction given below, measure the length to be piped.

Cut a length of bias strip, 1" (25mm) wide and slightly longer than the required measurement. Be extra generous with this length if there are corners or shaped edges included. Make any necessary joins to achieve the length required.

Fold the bias strip in half lengthways, with wrong sides together and press fold.

Cut a length of very narrow string and with small running stitches, encase the string in the fold. (The use of narrow string as opposed to soft cording allows you to stitch as close to the piping as possible, and achieve a much firmer rounded edging.)

Leave a length of string extending beyond each edge so that there will be no possibility of the string disappearing into the bias strip while you sew.

Trim one edge of seam allowance to 1/8" (3mm). Fold the other seam allowance in half and press turning.

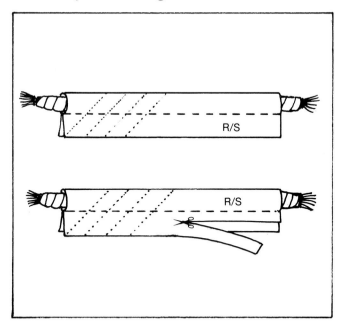

PIPING AN EDGE - continued

To attach the piping to a finished edge, hold the garment with the right side towards you and place the piping with the trimmed seam allowance towards you and lying against the wrong side of garment with the stitching line of encased piping even with the finished edge of garment.

With thread matching the piping, invisibly slipstitch the extended edge to the garment edge following the stitching line.

Turn the garment with the wrong side towards you and hem the turned edge of the remaining seam allowance to the inside to encase the trimmed edge. Take care not to stitch through to the right side.

At the beginning and end of attached piping where string has been left extended, cut string just inside casing. Curl ends over string and tuck away behind hem. Fasten ends securely.

To encase piping into an inner seam, place the piping to the right side of one edge of fabric having all raw edges even and tack in place just behind piped edge. With right sides together, place the other piece of fabric on top of piping, again matching raw edges. Turn the work to the other side so that you can see the tacking stitches holding the piping. Stitch on this line through all thicknesses. Press seam towards one side.

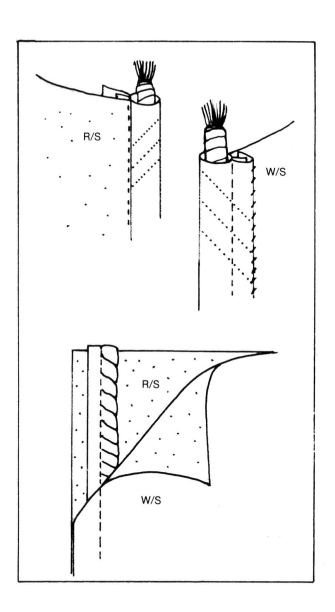

Sewing and Setting-in Sleeves

SEWING AND SETTING-IN SLEEVES

One piece sleeve into a bodice with normal shoulder and side seams

Join shoulder seams of bodice. Run 2 rows of gathers around sleeve head. If sleeve is a full gathered one, draw up gathers tightly and press over gathering threads to set gathers. (See Notes on Gathers)

Mark the centre of sleeve head and match to shoulder seam. Matching side edge of bodice parallel with sleeve underarm edge, pin sleeve head to armhole from underarm edge to where gathers start.

Ease out gathers to fit armhole. To be able to follow the curve of the top armhole and distribute the gathers more easily, hold the bodice armhole so that the sleeve is uppermost in your hand. Using the curve of your closed fingers as a base, pin the gathers in place. Tack armhole seam. Turn to right side and check that gathers are placed to your liking. Correct now if necessary and re-tack seam.

Stitch seam through centre of 2 rows of gathers so that the ridges of gathers are secured evenly; either by machine if the armhole is large enough, or by hand using back stitches for extra strength. Remove gathering threads and neaten raw edges of armhole seam.

With right sides together, join bodice side seam, sleeve and cuff (if applicable) in one operation, matching armhole ends and having armhole seam lying towards sleeve.

If applicable, either: Fold under cuff seam allowance to wrong side and hem over seam.

or: Narrow hem lower edge of sleeve and add narrow lace.

or: Finish sleeve as instructed in pattern, either while flat or at the end of construction.

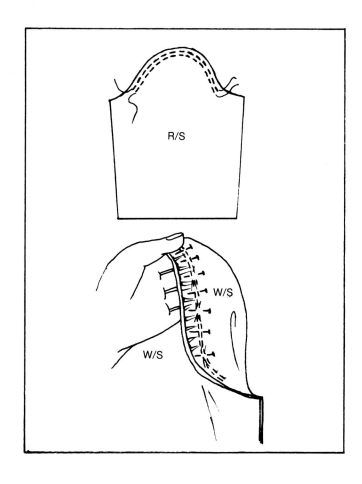

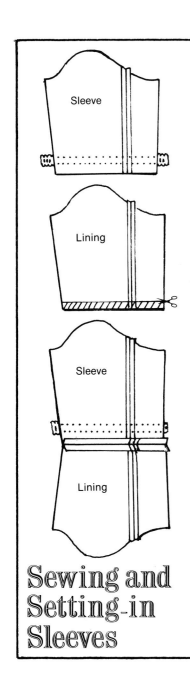

SEWING AND SETTING-IN SLEEVES - continued

A two part coat style sleeve with lining

The top and under sections of a two part coat sleeve are usually shaped so that sleeve head is more rounded above the back seam to allow movement within the more restricted outline of the sleeve and the front seam more curved to bring the sleeve towards the front of the garment. It is therefore important to recognise the left and right sleeve and ensure that the correct one is fitted into each armhole.

If the right and wrong side of your fabric is not easily identified, mark the right side of each section of sleeves and lining with a pin. This will help you avoid making up two left sleeves by mistake.

Join back seam of sleeve and lining separately.

Note

If the lower sleeve is to be decorated, apply lace, ribbon or braid while sleeve is now flat. Check that the decoration is of an even depth so that when the front seam is later joined the decoration will meet at the same point within the seam.

Cut off the seam allowance from the lower edge of the sleeve lining.

With right sides together, join sleeve to lining along lower edge.

With sleeve and lining out flat and right sides together, join front seam in one operation. Take care to match the wrist edge seam and also the edge of any decoration previously added.

Pull sleeve over lining, and with the raw edges even, tack sleeve and lining together around sleeve head. This will allow a small natural hem to form at lower edge and eliminate the need to hem the sleeve ends in such a restricted space.

Run a gathering thread along top of sleeve head between the front and back seams so that the fullness can be eased into the armhole at the shoulder line.

If it is preferred to fit the sleeve only into the armhole and hem lining over seam edge, do not tack the top edges together beforehand, and run a gathering line along sleeve and lining separately.

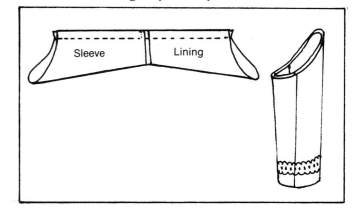

SEWING AND SETTING-IN SLEEVES - continued

To attach sleeve to bodice, mark the centre of the undersleeve and match this to the underarm seam of bodice. For shaped panels this could be the lower central point of bodice armhole. Pin sleeve to armhole up to front and back sleeve seams.

To be able to ease in the fullness of the sleeve head around the top of the armhole, hold the bodice armhole so that the sleeve is uppermost in your hand. Using the curve of your closed fingers as a base, pin sleeve to armhole using several pins close together to ease in fullness. Tack armhole seam. Press top of sleeve with a damp cloth to shrink out fullness. Turn to right side and check that sleeve fits armhole to your liking.

Correct now, if necessary, and re-tack.

Stitch seam either by machine, if armhole is large enough, or by hand using back stitches for extra strength. Remove tacking and gathering thread. Either oversew edges, or if lining has been kept separate, slipstitch lining over armhole seam, easing fullness at top.

Extra decoration can be added with slightly gathered lace or narrow pleating being stitched just inside wrist edge and extended beyond sleeve edge in proportion to the doll's arm.

A one piece sleeve with an elaborate oversleeve

There are generally three pattern pieces for the construction of this sleeve.

(1) A whole sleeve shape to be used as the base with a dotted line to indicate where the oversleeve will be fitted. This is normally cut from lining fabric.

(2) A lower sleeve shape to fit below dotted line.

(3) An exaggerated oversleeve shape to be pleated and tucked to fit upper sleeve lining.

Make pleats around sleeve head of oversleeve and tack to fit lining. Make tucks across lower edge and tack to lining along dotted line. At side edges make a downward facing tuck to take up fullness of oversleeve and so cause the exaggerated shape to form a horizontal tuck. If a more antique effect is required, arrange the centre fullness of the oversleeve to your liking and press folds firmly with a damp cloth.

Fold under seam allowance of top edge of lower sleeve. With right sides together, join lower sleeve to lining at wrist edge. Keeping sleeve and lining out flat and with right sides together, stitch underarm seam in one operation.

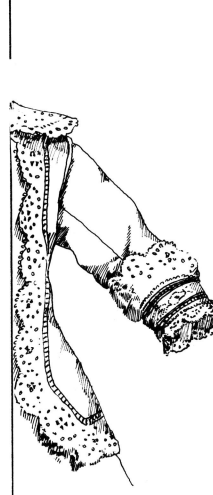

Sewing and Setting-in Sleeves

SEWING AND SETTING-IN SLEEVES - continued

Trim seam, and with right sides together, complete a French seam at side edge of oversleeve only, to encase raw edges.

Pull sleeve over lining and slipstitch top folded edge of lower sleeve over lower edge of oversleeve.

If the lower sleeve is to be decorated or a cuff added, this can either be carried out while the sleeve is flat or when the construction is completed.

To fit the sleeve into the bodice armhole, follow the same directions given for a one-piece sleeve at the beginning of this section.

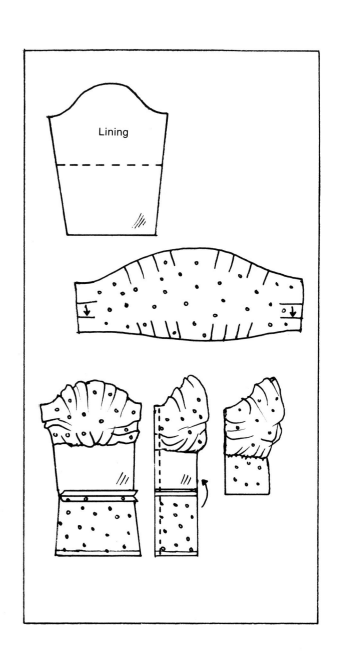

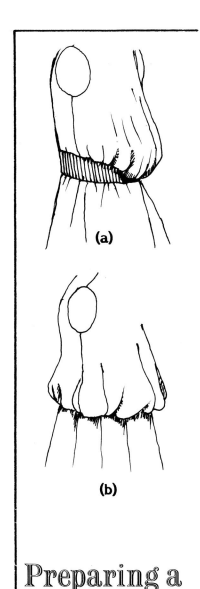

(a)

(b)

Preparing a Bloused Bodice

PREPARING A BLOUSED BODICE

Use the bodice pattern as the lining and prepare another pattern piece for the top bodice which is cut deeper by twice the depth of the required overlap to form a bloused effect.

The depth can **either** be kept centrally at the front with the back and sides normal length, when the pattern piece will look like Diagram (a) **or,** kept even across the whole width so that the fuller bloused effect will be all round the waist or dropped waist, when the pattern pieces will look like Diagram (b).

To make up (a) cut the new shaped front in dress fabric and tack to front lining, gathering in the lower fullness to fit lower edge and taking a downward facing tuck at side edges just above seam allowance. Cut identical back sections in dress fabric and tack to back lining.

Join side and shoulder seams in the normal way.

To make up (b) cut new front and back sections in dress fabric. Join side and shoulder seams of dress and lining separately. Turn and hem back opening facings of dress and lining separately.

With wrong sides together, tack dress and lining along raw edges of neck and armhole. Run a gathering line along lower edge of dress bodice and fit and tack to lower edge of lining, having back edges even, allowing fullness to fall down over lining.

When attaching bodice to skirt

Bodice can either be joined to a gathered decorated skirt or the bodice and skirt can be attached to a fitted band at a natural or dropped waistline.

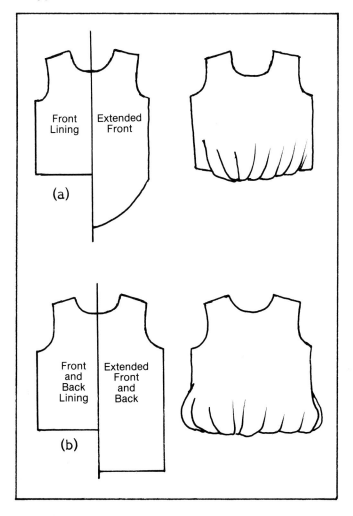

PREPARING A RUCHED PLASTRON FRONT

Using a bodice front pattern piece, allocate the space that you wish to decorate. Deepen the length if extra effect is required so that the plastron will overlap the skirt. Cut out the shape in a plain lining fabric to use as the base.

Measure the width at the widest point. If plain ruching is required, measure the depth and add up to 1" (2.5cm) for turnings at top. If tucks are also required, then decide on the sequence to be interspaced with ruching and add twice the depth of a tuck for each tuck added, to the original measurement of depth.

Cut a rectangle of dress or contrast fabric for the required width and depth. Turn under 1" (2.5cm) at top and ½" (1cm) at bottom and tack. Place a layer of lace to inside top edge to extend slightly above turning.

Stitch even running stitches across width of rectangle at 2cm intervals, with the first line holding the top turning and lace in place. Continue to end of depth. If tucks are to be included, space these between two rows of gathering lines and press them in alternate directions for extra effect.

While still flat, the top of the tucks can be decorated with further narrow lace, or if the tuck is deep enough it can be piped using the method for attaching to a prepared edge described on page (91).

Draw up the gathering lines evenly and fit to lining shape. Neaten top and bottom edges of lining and slipstich to turnings.

If the plastron is to be incorporated into a bodice allow side bodice sections to overlap neatened raw edges of plastron. If it is to be a separate piece and slipstitched inside a jacket style bodice, then bind the side edges of plastron. This will allow the fastenings more support when closing the jacket front at one side.

Very fine knife pleating can be added to lower edge of plastron to overlap skirt. Measure lower width and cut a strip of bias fabric three times the width plus seam allowances and twice the required depth. Fold the strip in half lengthways and wrong sides together. Neaten side edges. Pleat length as required. Stitch raw edges of pleating to wrong side of plastron behind lower turning.

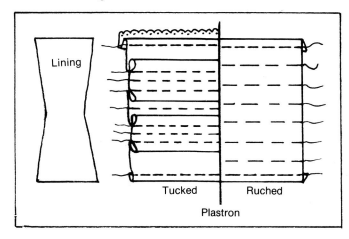

Lining

Tucked   Ruched

Plastron

DECORATIVE EDGINGS

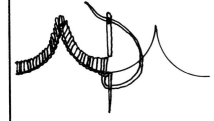

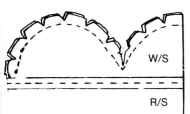

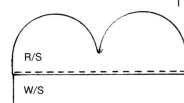

Decorative Edgings

Scalloped Edges

Scalloped edges can either be handstitched with close blanket stitches on a single fabric or machine stitched around marked semi circles using a folded hem or an extra facing strip.

Single fabric and handworked blanket stitch outline

Decide on the depth of each scallop and choose an appropriate coin or make a template in firm card.

Measure the greatest depth from the edge of fabric and draw a line on the wrong side. Place the coin or template to the right side edge of fabric and draw the semi circles along the whole width up to and even with the line drawn on the wrong side. Remember to have half semi circles at the joining edges and allow for your seam edges. Work blanket stitch around semi circles, neatly changing direction at each top curve.

Using sharp pointed scissors, trim away excess fabric from edge of scallops, taking care not to cut any of the stitching.

Double fabric and machine stitched scallops

Cut a facing strip of fabric a little more than the depth of each scallop and as long as needed. Turn under one long edge and hold turning with small running stitches. (A fully turned hem could be too bulky and mark across the scallops on the right side when pressing the final edge.)

With right sides together, place the raw edge of facing to the edge to be scalloped and tack in place.

With your coin or template, draw in the semi circles along the whole width. Again remember to have half semi circles at the joining edges and allow for your seam edges.

Using a small machine stitch, sew around the semi circle outline, pivoting at the top of each curve. Trim the excess fabric from the semi circle curves leaving the necessary seam allowance and snip into each top point, taking care not to cut the stitching.

Turn the facing to the wrong side and ease out the curves so that they all have a uniform outline. Press edges firmly.

Join the main seam and mitre back the seam edges at the centre curve.

If it is the bottom edge of a skirt that is being scalloped and it is wide enough to stitch the scalloped edges easily, then the main seam can be joined first. Ensure that the finished width will allow an equal amount of semi circles.

DECORATIVE EDGINGS - continued

Fagotting

Most modern machines have an extra attachment for creating a fagotting join but you may like to decorate your dress by hand.

Apart from being a decorative edging it is also useful for joining two sections of fabric together. It can be used with great effect when a sleeve or skirt needs to be lengthened.

The edges of the fabric to be joined must be in a finished state before decoration. Therefore either narrow hem or secure a turning with small running stitches.

Cut a slip of paper 2" (5cm) wide and as long as the two pieces of fabric being joined. Draw two parallel lines about $\frac{1}{4}$" (6mm) apart down the centre of the length of paper. Tack the finished edges of each fabric to each drawn line.

Fasten your matching or contrast embroidery thread at one end and work from left to right with slanting stitches from one edge to the other, pointing the needle towards the middle each time and sewing from the inside to the outside edge, having the thread pass over the previous slanting thread. Fasten thread securely. Remove paper and tacking thread carefully so as not to disturb the loose crossover threads.

Not only can the added piece of fabric be as deep as needed from a $\frac{1}{2}$" (1cm) edge to a 4" (10cm) border, but it can also be a decorative pre-stitched edging such as a rouleau tube which has been shell tucked, or a decorative braiding.

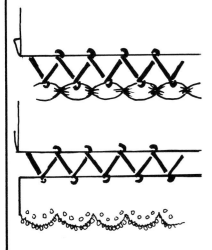

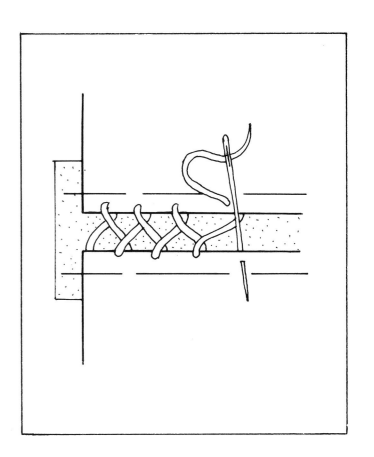

Decorative Edgings

99

DECORATIVE EDGINGS - continued

Shell Tucked Edging

This decorative edging is better used on fine fabrics and also fabrics which will not fray. Use a silk or embroidery thread of matching or toning colour for stitching.

Make a narrow hem and tack in place. With the wrong side of work facing you, fasten thread to the righthand side of work and run three small stitches through fold of hem without stitching through to the right side.

Take your needle over the fold and working from the right side to the wrong side, make 2 oversewing stitches and draw thread tightly. Work a further three running stitches into fold of hem and repeat the two oversewn stitches.

Repeat the process to the end of the hem.

The same decorative shell edging can be made down the fold of small tucks, around a neck binding or sleeve edge.

A shell tucked rouleau tube can not only be joined with a fagotting stitch as previously suggested and illustrated, but also can be used in place of braiding to decorate a cuff or the side edges of a jacket front or to cover the gathered edges of an applied lace frill.

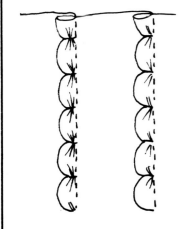

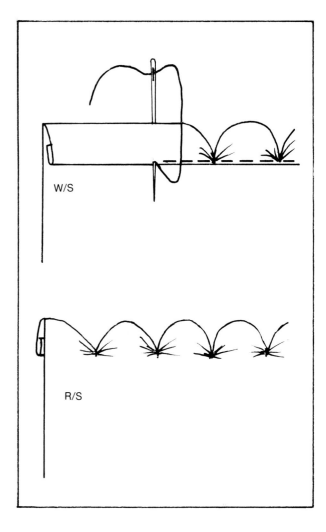

Decorative Edgings

100

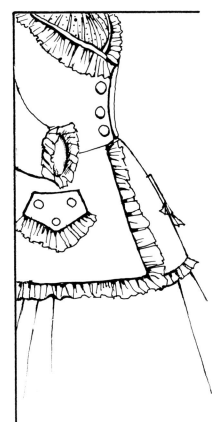

Decorative Edgings

DECORATIVE EDGINGS - continued

Decorative Applied Ribbon

Ribbon is a good substitute for braid when the latter is not found in the right width or colour.

Apply the ribbon straight and only attach it along its top edge allowing the ribbon to fall free over the fabric. Sometimes if you stitch both edges to the fabric, you can pucker either the ribbon or the underneath fabric, or even both as the different textures of ribbon and fabric pull against each other.

Ribbon can also be gathered up with small running stitches in a variety of ways to create varying designs. Always ensure that the running stitches are continuous and no back stitches have been made inadvertently, to prevent the thread being pulled tight.

(1)   Running stitches along each side of corded edge.

(2)   Running stitches along centre of ribbon.

(3)   Running stitches made diagonally from one edge to another, making sure that the edge stitch carries over the corded edge at each turn of direction.

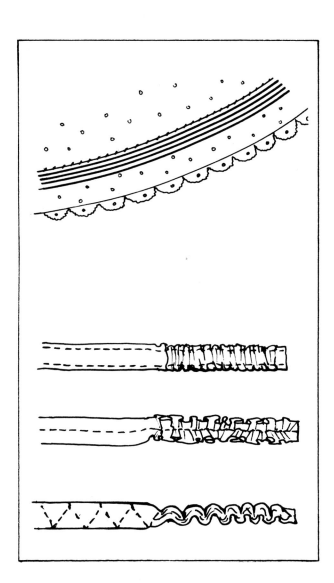

DECORATIVE EDGINGS - continued

Rosettes

Cut a length of ribbon between 6" (15cm) to 10" (25cm) depending on the width being gathered.

Secure thread at one edge and run small stitches just inside corded edge. Pull up tightly to form a curled circle. Fasten thread securely. Ribbon ends can be oversewn on the wrong side or overlapped and slipstiched. A smaller rosette made of narrower ribbon can be set in the middle of a larger rosette, for extra effect.

Looped Rosettes

Cut a small 1" (2cm) square of fabric. Fold it in half and half again to make a ½" (1cm) square to be used as the base on which to stitch the ribbon loops. Stitch in centre to hold in place.

Starting in the centre of this base, stitch end of ribbon to centre and deciding on the length of loops, fold ribbon and stitch again at the centre. Continue around base overlapping ribbon loops until circle is completed. Fasten a bead or small pearl in the centre of looped rosette.

Ribbon Bows

There is often a need for a decorative flat ribbon bow which has not resulted from two ends of a sash or threaded ribbon being tied together.

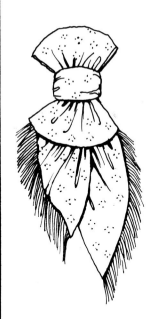

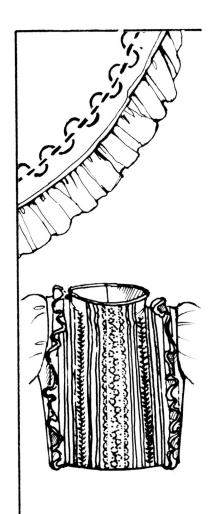

DECORATIVE EDGINGS - continued

Decorative Stitches

There will always be an occasion when hand worked embroidery stitches will be needed.

Use embroidery thread, either with two or three strands and choose a toning or contrast colour.

Embroidery stitches can be used between the vertical tucks of a yoke, or to apply insertion lace to a bodice or skirt.

To decorate the neck binding or outline a small cuff.

Underwear will always be enhanced with the addition of embroidery stitches especially feather stitching.

None of these stitches illustrated here are difficult and if you have not tried them before, practice on a piece of sheeting. You will soon find you can keep the stitches even and in proportion to the scale of the garment as well as the size and length of the area being embroidered.

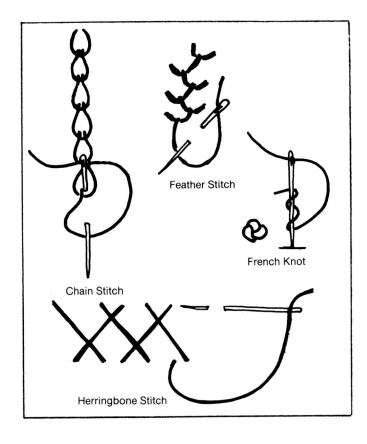

Feather Stitch

French Knot

Chain Stitch

Herringbone Stitch

Decorative Edgings

DECORATING HATS

Whether you are making an individual hat for your doll out of fabric to match her dress, or covering a hat shape, or assembling a hat with plaited straw, it will certainly need some decoration. Flowers, feathers, ribbons, braid, lace and even dress fabric cut on the cross to be used instead of ribbons, are all possibilities for hat decoration.

Artificial flowers can be bought singly or in sprays of small flowers which can also be divided and used singly for very small hats. Silk flowers can often be found in florist shops or the bridal counter when the pastel colours could be just the right shade. Try to avoid the flowers that have been excessively stiffened and also discard the plastic leaves and stems that are included in some flower sprays. Alternatively, you could make your own silk flowers using small offcuts from the dress fabric so that the whole outfit will be colour co-ordinated.

Feathers can be bought in a variety of sizes and colours. The length and width of a feather should always be in proportion to the size of the hat as well as the doll's face. If you are placing a feather in a more upright position on the hat, check also that the total height will not overpower the doll. It is still possible to find old feathers in a charity or second-hand shop and these will be ideal for decorating an antique doll's hat.

Ribbons are perhaps the most useful decoration for a hat, as well as being used functionally for fastening the hat under the doll's chin. Narrow ribbons can be tied in small individual bows and stitched between the layers of frills framing the front of a mob cap or bonnet or set in amongst the flowers nestling behind the brim of a more formal hat.

When making bows from wider ribbon, make sure that the loops of the bow will be in proportion to the width of the ribbon and yet not be too big to overpower the hat. Ribbons can be gathered along one side of the selvedge to form small rosettes. They can also be gathered in various directions to form ruching lengths to decorate the outer edge of a high brim, or to neaten the neck edge or any other raw edges when a bulky hem would be out of place.

When a narrow pleated brim is called for and the hat fabric would prove too bulky, use a toning or contrast ribbon. Trim off one selvedge edge from the side to be included into the crown seam to allow more flexibility around the curve, keeping the other selvedge edge to form a neat finish to the brim. If however, you are unable to find the right ribbon in the width or colour you need, and providing the matching dress fabric is fine enough, cut out strips of dress fabric cut on the cross to use as ribbons. Either narrow hem or use the overlocking stitch of your sewing machine on the finest setting to neaten the raw edges, or alternatively, fold the length double and stitch together to form a tubing.

Decorating
Hats

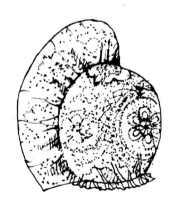

Turn tubing to right side and press so that the seam will be placed in the centre of the 'wrong' side.

You can co-ordinate your dress and hat by adding the same braid you have used to decorate the dress, around the brim or to highlight some special feature of the hat shape. Like ribbon, braid is also useful for covering the raw edges of applied gathered or pleated fabric or for holding added lace in place.

Lace can soften and enhance even the simplest of hat shapes. Larger widths of lace or net can be cut the same shape as the hat crown and laid over the main fabric. Study the design of the lace and keep it central over the crown, tack in place around the outer edges and treat as one fabric.

Brims can also be covered in lace. If the lace is wide enough to fold in half lengthways, place the outer edge of brim into the fold and pleat the excess fullness towards the inner curve of either side. If the lace is only the width of one side of brim, apply the lace to the front only placing the scalloped edge around the outer edge.

For a high brimmed hat, the brim will need to be decorated after it has been assembled but before it is joined to the hat crown. It is usually only the front of the brim that is decorated.

To decorate the brim with a single length of lace, ensure that the width is the same or larger than the measurement of the centre front height. Measure the outer curve and cut the length to match. Mark the length in half and place the centre to the centre of brim with the scalloped edge even or slightly overlapping the outer curve. Working from the centre to either side, pin the lace edge in place. Return to the centre and pull the lace taut to the inner edge and pin in place. Continue to pin the lace to the inner edge from centre to either side, overlapping and slanting the fullness towards the centre. Cut off the excess lace at the inner edges. If the wide lace has a distinctive design which you wish to show to full advantage, ease only the slightest fullness towards the inner curve keeping the centre front as flat as possible.

If you are unable to use wide lace, you can attach narrower lace in layers overlapping each consecutive row until the brim is covered. Start at the outer edge of brim and lap each layer over the previous one to hide the stitching line. The layers of lace can either be pleated or gathered to allow for the curve of the brim.

A high brim hat can also be decorated with silk in a contrast or toning colour. Cut a length of fabric up to three times the measurement of the outer curve of the brim, with the width equal to the height at the centre front.

Decorating Hats

DECORATING HATS - continued

Pleat the length with either knife or box pleats, and press. Place the top of the pleated length even with the outer curve fixing with pins pointing outwards. Run a gathering thread along the lower edge and draw up fullness to fit inner edge of brim. Tack the pleating in place at inner edge and cut away the excess at either end. Cover the raw edge of pleating around outer curve with braid or ruched ribbon or bind the edge with the main hat fabric, cut on the cross. Remove the pins after decoration has been completed.

A beret with a headband will not require elaborate decoration but corded ribbon just narrower than the headband depth can be attached to the headband when completed. Stitch the ribbon to the headband along one edge only and allow the other edge to fall free. This will prevent the headband from puckering when the ribbon and headband fabric could pull against each other, and also allow the natural stretch of the headband to fit over the doll's head without restriction. A flat bow can be added to hide the ribbon join. A decorative tassle can be attached to the centre crown and allowed to fall to one side when the beret is worn.

A sailor beret can either be decorated in the same way or similar cotton tape used to decorate the collar and cuffs of the sailor jacket can be added to the headband. A useful alternative to cotton tape is the narrow cotton stockinette tubing which is currently available from wool shops for specialised knitting and comes in a variety of colours. It is very flexible especially when going round those corners of a sailor collar.

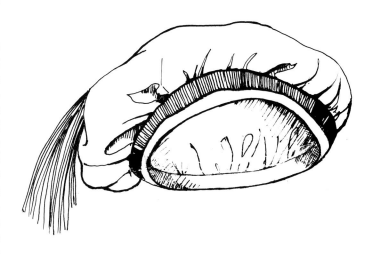

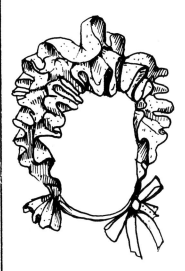

Decorating Hats

Index